Sport Culture

Editor: Tina Brand

Volume 341

Independence Educational Publishers

First published by Independence Educational Publishers

The Studio, High Green

Great Shelford

Cambridge CB22 5EG

England

ISBN-13: 978 1 86168 792 0

Printed in Great Britain

Zenith Print Group

Contents

Introduction

SPORT CULTURE is Volume 341 in the **ISSUES** series. The aim of the series is to offer current, diverse information about important issues in our world, from a UK perspective.

ABOUT SPORT CULTURE

Sport is a part of many people's lives, whether they are participants in sport or spectators. This book explores the many issues which sport raises, such as violence amongst football fans, discrimination against women in sport, and the issue of doping in sport. It also considers the impact of Olympic success which has caused a surge in youngsters taking up sport for the first time. It also looks at such issues as new technology in sport, the rise in ticket prices and women's role in sport.

OUR SOURCES

Titles in the **ISSUES** series are designed to function as educational resource books, providing a balanced overview of a specific subject.

The information in our books is comprised of facts, articles and opinions from many different sources, including:

⇨ Newspaper reports and opinion pieces

⇨ Website factsheets

⇨ Magazine and journal articles

⇨ Statistics and surveys

⇨ Government reports

⇨ Literature from special interest groups.

A NOTE ON CRITICAL EVALUATION

Because the information reprinted here is from a number of different sources, readers should bear in mind the origin of the text and whether the source is likely to have a particular bias when presenting information (or when conducting their research). It is hoped that, as you read about the many aspects of the issues explored in this book, you will critically evaluate the information presented.

It is important that you decide whether you are being presented with facts or opinions. Does the writer give a biased or unbiased report? If an opinion is being expressed, do you agree with the writer? Is there potential bias to the 'facts' or statistics behind an article?

ASSIGNMENTS

In the back of this book, you will find a selection of assignments designed to help you engage with the articles you have been reading and to explore your own opinions. Some tasks will take longer than others and there is a mixture of design, writing and research-based activities that you can complete alone or in a group.

Useful weblinks

www.esrc.ukri.org

www.gov.uk

www.independent.co.uk

www.independent.ie

www.inews.co.uk

www.nhs.uk

www.ox.ac.uk

www.parliament.uk

www.sportengland.org

www.sport80.com

www.telegraph.co.uk

www.theconversation.com

www.thegolfbusiness.co.uk

www.theguardian.com

www.uksport.gov.uk

www.yougov.co.uk

FURTHER RESEARCH

At the end of each article we have listed its source and a website that you can visit if you would like to conduct your own research. Please remember to critically evaluate any sources that you consult and consider whether the information you are viewing is accurate and unbiased.

New Olympic and Paralympic sports to receive National Lottery funding as more medals across more sports targeted in Tokyo 2020

⇨ Increased investment in Olympic sports of over £1 million to fund medal potential athletes in new Tokyo events.

⇨ Increased investment in new Paralympic medal events of over £2 million to strengthen our medal ambitions including funding para taekwondo, para badminton and para canoeing Va'a boat classes.

⇨ Over £2.5 million for new innovative medal support plans to provide National Lottery funding to world-level athletes in Badminton, Archery, Karate and Sport Climbing.

⇨ Tokyo Olympic medal target range increased to 54–92 (from 51–85).

⇨ Tokyo Paralympic medal target range increased to 119–168 (from 115–162).

UK Sport today announced new investment into more British medal hopes and exciting new events and disciplines in the Tokyo 2020 Olympics and Paralympics.

The high-performance funding agency revealed as part of its annual investment review that athletes in Para Taekwondo, Para Badminton, Sport Climbing, Karate and BMX Freestyle will all receive National Lottery support as they enter the Olympic and Paralympic programme for the first time.

British athletes in all five events have been judged to have genuine medal potential as UK Sport continues its mission to inspire the nation with more medals and more medallists in Tokyo than Rio 2016, and now in more sports too.

In the new Paralympic sports, world champion Para Taekwondo fighter Amy Truesdale will lead the charge in Tokyo, while in Para Badminton the British squad showed their potential at the 2017 World Championships and will now receive National Lottery funding to develop their World Class Programme.

In BMX Freestyle the call has gone out to find new talent to represent Britain in the discipline and compete alongside proven performers Alex Coleborn and Charlotte Worthington

as part of British Cycling's world class programme, with additional investment to develop the BMX freestyle programme in the East Midlands.

Initial investment in the new Olympic sports will be made through new innovative and targeted medal support plans, as part of a new UK Sport investment stream aimed at specific athletes with immediate medal potential in Tokyo. In combined Sport Climbing this will initially support current bouldering world champion Shauna Coxsey, and in Karate it will support 2016 world champion Jordan Thomas, so that they can go for gold in Tokyo 2020.

Following strong results in 2017, the UK Sport Board has also decided to invest in similar targeted medal

Sport	Funding type		
	WCP	APA	Total
Archery	£630,000	TBC	£630,000
Athletics	£23,007,531	£3,911,500	£26,919,031
Badminton*	£630,000	TBC	£630,000
Boxing	£12,084,436	£2,183,917	£14,268,353
Canoeing	£16,544,693	£2,578,500	£19,123,193
Cycling	£24,759,306	£4,864,958	£29,624,264
Diving	£7,252,184	£1,599,042	£8,851,226
Equestrian	£12,671,105	£1,828,458	£14,499,653
Gymnastics	£13,811,036	£2,646,917	£16,457,953
Hockey	£12,723,612	£4,401,708	£17,125,320
Judo	£6,564,334	£830,833	£7,395,167
Karate	£630,000	TBC	£630,000
Modern Pentathlon	£5,498,321	£642,208	£6,140,529
Rowing	£24,706,762	£5,817,833	£30,524,595
Sailing	£22,249,000	£3,508,417	£25,757,417
Shooting	£6,008,790	£6,008,790	£6,943,332
Sport Climbing	£630,000	TBC	£630,000
Swimming	£18,812,421	£3,618,417	£22,430,838
Taekwondo	£8,223,805	£1,615,108	£9,838,913
Triathlon	£7,049,372	£1,019,333	£8,068,705
Total	**£224,486,798**	**£42,001,691**	**£266,488,489**

Tokyo Paralympic funding figures

Sport	WCP	APA	Total
Boccia	£3,071,203	£708,458	£3,779,661
Disability Shooting	£2,076,000	£423,000	£2,499,000
Para-Archery	£2,719,092	£1,037,000	£3,756,092
Para-Athletics	£8,937,070	£3,723,667	£12,660,737
Para-Badminton	£960,000	£277,500	£1,237,500
Para-Canoe	£3,017,671	£862,250	£3,879,921
Para-Cycling	£5,638,328	£2,456,125	£8,094,453
Para-Equestrian Dressage	£3,294,056	£1,067,583	£4,361,639
Para-Rowing	£2,614,482	£1,050,083	£3,644,565
Para-Swimming	£8,846,263	£2,023,333	£10,869,596
Para-Table Tennis	£2,726,060	£913,333	£3,639,593
Para-Taekwondo	£435,000	£84,000	£519,000
Para-Triathlon	£2,852,775	£907,000	£3,759,775
Powerlifting	£1,097,075	£218,417	£1,315,492
VI Judo	£1,968,986	£72,000	£2,040,986
Wheelchair Basketball	£4,603,219	£2,595,125	£7,198,344
Wheelchair Fencing	£637,472	£311,750	£949,222
Wheelchair Rugby	£50,000	–	£50,000
Wheelchair Tennis	–	£633,250	£633,250
Total Paralympic	**£55,544,752**	**£19,363,874**	**£74,908,626**

PyeongChang Olympic funding

	Funding amount
Bobsleigh	£5,003,476
Curling	£5,655,150
Figure Skating	£1,235,593
Short Track	£4,764,006
Skeleton	£6,549,617
Ski and Snowboard	£5,003,476
Total	**£28,353,135**

PyeongChang Paralympic funding

	Funding amount
Para-Ski and Snowboard	£2,771,456
Wheelchair Curling	£1,137,767
Total	**£3,909,223**

Source: UK Sport

support plans in Badminton and Archery for individual athletes with proven world championship-level success in the current Olympic cycle. In Badminton this investment will support Chris and Gabby Adcock, who won a bronze medal in the mixed doubles at the World Championships in Glasgow last year. And in Archery it will support Patrick Huston and Naomi Folkard, who achieved a bronze medal in the new mixed team event at the 2017 World Championships in Mexico. Potentially this medal support plan investment could reach up to eight athletes in each sport with funding for full-time training as well as coaching, competitions, travel, equipment and expert sport science and medicine.

The British Wheelchair Rugby team – which won European Gold in 2017 – will also receive a small amount of transitional funding to support its ambitions to attend the World Championships in Australia this year to allow them to prove their Tokyo medal potential.

Other exciting new chances for medals in Tokyo will include the return of the Madison in Track Cycling, the new Triathlon Mixed Relay, and the Para Canoe Va'a boat classes. In total, 13 more Olympic podium-level athletes and 28 more Paralympic podium-level athletes can be funded by the National Lottery so that the next generation of sports fans can be inspired again.

Overall this means UK Sport is increasing its medal ambitions for Tokyo within its existing budget, following a successful performance year in 2017 which surpassed the achievements in the equivalent stages of the London 2012 and Rio 2016 cycles. The Tokyo Olympic medal target range is increasing to 54–92 (from 51–85) and the Paralympic medal target range is increasing to 119–168 (from 115–162).

The increased investments have been made possible as a result of releasing previously ring-fenced funding for new sports and disciplines now assessed to have medal potential in Tokyo; and governing bodies such as those for sailing and athletics increasing their co-contribution to funding their world class programmes either from other sources of income or by finding efficiencies, meaning money can be reallocated to more sports. Karate and Para Taekwondo will also share world class facilities and expertise with the existing GB Taekwondo squad in Manchester's Sport City, in the latest example of the high-performance system working together to support each other and save money.

Matt Hancock, Secretary of State for Digital, Culture, Media and Sport, said:

'Britain is an Olympic and Paralympic powerhouse and this funding announcement shows the depth of medal potential we have across a diverse range of sports.

'Sustained investment from National Lottery players and the Government has been fundamental to Team GB and ParalympicsGB's success. It is fantastic news that the likes of BMX, Para Taekwondo and Sport Climbing are now also receiving support to give our athletes the best chance to win medals at Tokyo 2020, make the country proud and inspire many to get involved in sport.'

UK Sport Chief Executive Liz Nicholl said:

'UK Sport's vision is to inspire the nation through Olympic and Paralympic success. Today's announcement, following the annual investment review into our summer sports, confirms strong potential to deliver more medal moments from more sports in Tokyo 2020.

'Exciting new events such as Sport Climbing, Karate, Para Taekwondo and BMX freestyle will be funded to inspire a whole new generation of Olympic and Paralympic sports fans and it is fantastic that we already have world class talents ready to compete for medals in those events and more.

'We are also delighted to be able to target funding to medal potential athletes who have delivered success at a world championship level in 2017 in the cases of badminton and archery. Thanks to National Lottery and taxpayer support we have been able to fund more sports targeting medal success in Tokyo than ever before with the promise of more British athletes on the Olympic and Paralympic podium to inspire the nation.'

Today's announcement means that UK Sport will be targeting medals in 20 Olympic sports and 18 Paralympic sports in Tokyo 2020. This is more than the equivalent UK Sport-funded medals won in London 2012 and Rio 2016 (excluding non-UK Sport-funded sports such as tennis, golf and Rugby 7s).

New co-funding contribution agreements include Athletics and Para Athletics receiving £430,000 less from UK Sport, including £180,000 of overhead efficiencies; and Sailing receiving £116,000 less due to an increase in co-funding contribution. The Para Taekwondo and Karate programmes will also be based at the National Taekwondo Centre in Sport City in Manchester, an elite training centre also supported by Sport England and Manchester City Council. This will allow athletes to collaborate and share resources and expertise with the elite GB Taekwondo squad in a partnership supported by the British Karate Federation.

1 February 2018

⇨   The above information is reprinted with kind permission from UK Sport. Please visit www.uksport.gov.uk for further information.

NHS health check

Health and fitness trackers

From lowering blood pressure and cholesterol to tackling obesity and smoking, digital technology is transforming the way you can manage and improve your health.

Apps and other digital tools are effective ways to share your goals, get advice and support, or talk to other people who can inspire you with their experiences.

Wearable fitness gadgets

Wearable fitness devices are designed to automatically track things like your physical activity, sleep patterns, mood and calorie intake.

These gadgets, which come in the form of wristbands, watches and earphones, can be a good option if you need a nudge and want information about your well-being – but they do come at a cost.

Many other online tools and apps are free, easy to use and can be accessed on a smartphone, such as an Android or iPhone, or a desktop computer.

The following tools and apps can help you lower your risk of developing the conditions that the NHS Health Check looks out for.

Quit smoking

Smokefree

This app is designed to help you quit smoking over 28 days. It provides daily tips, advice and support, and you'll be rewarded for meeting goals.

If you stay smokefree for the 28-day programme, you're up to five times more likely to quit for good.

Price: Free

Reduce your drinking

Alcohol unit calculators

Regularly drinking more than 14 units of alcohol a week risks harming your health.

Alcohol apps let you check how much alcohol you're drinking and

the number of calories you're putting away, too.

Price: Free

Lose weight

NHS weight loss plan

With up to four million downloads to date, the NHS weight loss plan has helped thousands of people with their weight loss goals.

The 12-week plan combines calorie counting and exercise to help you lose weight safely and sustainably.

The plan is delivered through 12 fun and motivating weight loss packs, which include a colourful food and activity log sheet.

You can also get advice and support from the Health Unlocked online Weight Loss community.

Price: Free

Healthy eating

One You Easy Meals

The One You Easy Meals recipes app is a great free way of helping everybody eat tasty healthier meals.

Use it to search for easy calorie-counted recipes for breakfast, lunch, evening meals and puddings.

Keep track with the handy shopping list, which organises the ingredients you need by supermarket aisle, and learn more about being food smart and making healthier choices.

Price: Free

Calorie checker

Use the NHS calorie checker to look up the calories of more than 150,000 different food and drink items.

Its database lists the calorie and fat content of:

⇨ generic foods

⇨ branded products

⇨ meals from around the world

⇨ alcoholic drinks

⇨ restaurant meals, including fast-food chains.

For quick access to the calorie checker on the go, save the page to your mobile device's home screen and use it just like an app.

Price: Free

Change4Life Sugar Smart

Many of us eat and drink too much sugar without realising it. The Change4Life Sugar Smart app lets you scan the bar code and food and drink labels to see how much total sugar they contain.

That way you can make healthier choices when shopping for food and cut your sugar intake.

Price: Free

Improve your fitness

Couch to 5K running podcasts

The NHS Couch to 5K plan is designed to get you off the sofa and running 5km in just nine weeks.

This gradual running plan is a free and easy way of getting fitter and healthier, and has helped tens of thousands of people so far.

The plan is delivered through a series of podcasts that can be downloaded to any mobile device, and is supported by the Health Unlocked online Couch to 5K community.

Price: Free

You can also try the One You Couch to 5K app

Strength and Flex podcasts

The Strength and Flex plan is a five-week exercise programme delivered through five podcasts.

The plan is a fun way of improving your strength and flexibility, and getting you motivated to exercise regularly.

If you're not very active, don't enjoy exercise, need a bit of a push, or simply want a way to get fit again, Strength and Flex is for you.

Price: Free

NHS Fitness Studio

Not technically an app or tracker, but a great free online resource, the NHS Fitness Studio has more than 20 free exercise videos for all abilities.

They range from aerobics and belly dancing to pre- and postnatal yoga, as well as exercises suitable for people with limited mobility.

Price: Free

3 August 2018

⇨ The above information is reproduced with kind permission from the NHS. Please visit www. nhs.uk for further information.

Busting three myths around elite sports performance

An article from **The Conversation.**

By Tim Rees, Professor in Sport, Bournemouth University

THE CONVERSATION

Creating high-performance sportspeople is something like alchemy, and comes with the same baggage of half-thoughts, assumptions and quasi-quackery. But the research has moved on, and we can put to bed three powerful myths about building the ultimate athlete.

The first of these myths is linked to the idea that 'practice makes perfect'. This message has been passed down through generations as a fact and there is now much popular wisdom and misinformation, derived from a belief in a simplified number: 10,000 hours. But can it really be that easy? There is no question sportspeople must practise a lot to get to the top. But how much is enough? And can we all be world class with sufficient practice?

The 10,000 hours 'rule' came out of work by a psychologist at Florida State University, Anders Ericsson. Popularised in books such as *Bounce* by Matthew Syed, and *Outliers* by Malcolm Gladwell, it has led to the belief that if you put in this amount of deliberate and focused practice you can reach elite levels of performance.

Golden chance

But rather than needing 10,000 hours, there is now evidence that as few as 4,400 hours of deliberate practice may be sufficient to claim a gold medal in hockey, 4,500 hours to reach a top-tier European national football side, and just 4,000 hours to reach the highest levels in basketball and netball. Good news, then, for those with busy lives but a hankering for Olympic success.

Ericsson himself has emphasised that he did not intend a 'rule' to be drawn from his research. He does though for the most part believe that practice is more important than genetics but would no doubt agree that to make it as a rower or basketball player, way above average height and limb length are a clear advantage.

And there is also intriguing evidence that genetics may more generally influence one's suitability for endurance versus power events. Genetics may underpin key performance factors such as explosive strength, speed of movement, running speed, reaction time, flexibility and balance.

Therefore, although we can't predict the world's best athletes based on genetics, combinations of gene variants are likely to act in concert to influence the sport in which athletes are most likely to successfully compete. It is at that point that practice comes into play.

Developing a theme

The second myth is that you must be in a sport's development programme from an early age to make it. Here I'd offer a cautionary tale to parents who feel pressured to drag their offspring all over the country to attend development squads, fearing this is the only route to the top.

The sporting landscape is littered with those who have relocated in pursuit of success never to fulfil their early promise, while at the same time halting opportunities for the development of other key attributes necessary for performance and life.

Although most world class sportspeople have been involved in athlete support programmes at some stage, the evidence suggests a very non-linear path to the top. There is frequent selection and de-selection from squads, rather than linear progression within

athlete support programmes. But here's the conundrum: while most talent identification systems use current junior performance as the main criterion for selection to a development programme, junior success does not reliably predict long-term senior success.

Longitudinal studies with large samples of athletes across numerous sports have shown that the younger the first recruitment to a support programme, the younger the exit from the programme, and the higher the level of senior success, the later the age of first recruitment on to programmes.

In other words, the world's best performers are recruited to support programmes significantly later than their less-able counterparts. It's important to stress then that early athlete support programmes are not the sole route to the development of talent. And furthermore, the world's best sportspeople tend not to have progressed exclusively within one sport, but have practised multiple sports during childhood and adolescence.

In fact, the probability of attaining the highest level in sport is likely enhanced by the coupling of a large volume of intensive, organised specific training in the main sport with appreciable amounts of organised training and competitions in other sports.

Role models

The third myth is the concept of the happy, successful, champion that we should admire. The world's best athletes are extraordinary, and we rightly marvel at their prowess and bask in their glory. Holding them up as role models to create a sporting and physical activity legacy is laudable.

But with 307 golds available at Rio 2016 for a world population of 7.4 billion, Olympic champions are, by definition, abnormal. In fact, there is now growing recognition that the intense resilience, determination, and will to win of the world's best performers can be driven by something altogether different from happiness. The cartoon strip Dilbert facetiously observed: 'I would think that a willingness to practise the same thing for 10,000 hours is a mental disorder.' At the very least, it takes a certain mindset to cope and flourish in the harsh world of elite sport.

In fact, there is emerging evidence that this deep-seated need to win at all costs may be driven by early developmental adversity and obstacles, which leave an indelible mark on the sportsperson. Thus, although this level of determination and commitment is something we might rightly be in awe of, to think we could or should emulate it is unrealistic, unnecessary and potentially damaging.

The route to the top in sport isn't as simple as accrued hours or neat pathways. It likely entails many ups and downs both within and outside sport. We should beware a tendency to over-simplify past success, and in doing so, leave the door open to a renewed appreciation for the myriad ways in which elite level can be reached.

13 March 2017

⇨ The above information is reprinted with kind permission from *The Conversation*. Please visit www.theconversation.com for further information.

Beyond the violence, the shocking power the ultras wield over Italian football

April's thuggery in Liverpool highlighted a subculture with a dark and deadly side.

By Tobias Jones

The grim violence outside Anfield on Tuesday night, in which Roma fans attacked their Liverpool counterparts, was like a flashback to the dark days of the 1980s: *romanisti* were carrying belts, bottles, stones and even a hammer; one man, 53-year-old Sean Cox, remains in a coma.

Although it seemed like the hooliganism of old, its roots are actually very different. The Roma fans are part of what Italians call 'ultras', meaning 'beyond', 'intransigent' or 'extreme'. Every Italian football team has its ultra gang and big clubs have dozens. I've been researching the subculture for years and, violence apart, they're nothing like old-school British thugs.

Hooligans were generally chaotic and drunk. Italy's ultras are uber organised, hierarchical and calculating. They started, in the late 1960s and early 1970s, as wannabe paramilitary groups. They gave themselves names that made them sound like insurgents: Commandos, Guerrillas and Fedayeen (the group suspected of Tuesday's violence). Although nominally apolitical, the vast majority of ultra groups in the 1970s borrowed the images and slogans of the far left, some even using the names of partisan brigades from the Second World War.

That paramilitary planning is evident in the weekly meeting each ultra group has in its own HQ, with a 'president' or *capo* taking charge of proceedings. I've sat in on many and they're like strategic policy meetings, with the core members debating slogans, songs, press releases, alliances and ambushes. I once asked someone nicknamed 'Half-a-kilo' what would happen if I started my own song on the terraces and he was aghast at such spontaneity: 'It would be a very serious offence if it hadn't been agreed by the directive.'

So it was no surprise that last week's ultras were dressed identically: all in black bomber jackets, blue jeans and white trainers. As with many Italians, the ultras are fixated on appearance and pageantry: for major games, they spend tens of thousands of euros on what they call 'choreographies': stadium mosaics, taunts, flags and flares. An ultra group's own banner is like a military herald.

In that sense, the ultra world seems folkloric: the ultra world is a faux-mediaeval defence of the country's *campanilismo* (attachment to the local bell tower). In fact, many ultras say they care nothing about football: it's all about territorial defence, about the colours, the fights and the 'mentality'. Ask an ultra next to you on the terraces who scored a goal and they'll laugh at such naivety: they either weren't watching or players change teams so often that they don't know or care about the name.

It's a world that, at its best, can often seem like a Sherwood Forest of outlaws and rebels. Their hated 'Sheriff of Nottingham' is modern football: the fixture folly caused by TV schedules, tinny stadium music, Orwellian surveillance, disloyal players and asset-stripping owners. Many ultra groups from small clubs are genuinely noble, racing to help earthquake and flood victims or planting trees after forest fires.

But there's also a very dark side. Last December, Italy's parliamentary anti-mafia commission concluded in a report on the phenomenon that ultra behaviour 'often reproduces mafia methods': *omertà* (silence or secretiveness), collecting funds for jailed accomplices and holding weapons and drugs for third parties. The head of Lazio's *Irriducibili* was recently convicted of dealing hundreds of kilos of cocaine in the capital. The commission's report suggested that 30% of ultras are either petty or major-league criminals.

Dealing in tickets is as lucrative as, and less risky than, slinging drugs. Until his arrest, one Juventus capo-ultra, a Sicilian member of the Bravi Ragazzi (the 'goodfellas') was making €30,000 (£26,000) a game through ticket touting. That was only possible because Juventus were giving bulk tickets to ultra groups to keep them sweet; the ultras made millions a year and the club were untroubled by bad behaviour that might have meant fines or docked points. Few clubs can afford to take on their ultras – a fans' strike is costly – with the result that there are always compromises between the suits and the 'soldiers'.

When I went, a year ago, to the HQ of Juventus' Droogs (named after the violent types in *A Clockwork Orange*), I saw bricks of cash and tickets next to a huge poster of Mussolini. It was more like a bank than a fan club. The Calabrian mafia tried to move in on those huge profits and in 2016 the man acting as a bridge between the ultras and the club, Ciccio Bucci, either committed suicide or was 'suicided' the day after talking to investigators. His was just the most recent in a long line of deaths; over the years, the ultras have been responsible for shootings, arson, stabbings and disappearances. Each time, the murderer is eulogised on the terraces. At Anfield on Tuesday, one of the banners held by Roma fans read 'DDS Con Noi', meaning 'Daniele De Santis is with us'. De Santis murdered a Napoli fan before the Italian cup final in 2014. Two years ago, an ultra in Fermo, in Le Marche, murdered a Nigerian immigrant and his name was sung throughout every subsequent match.

In the past, only a handful of ultra groups (those of Lazio, Verona and Inter, for example) were from the far right. Now the vast majority have neo-fascist names, symbols, slogans and salutes: Hitler and Mussolini are frequently invoked and foreigners are abhorred. In 2012, Tottenham fans were stabbed in Rome as they were considered Jewish. Anne Frank stickers have been used to insult rival teams. Hopefully, Liverpool fans won't have any trouble during the return leg in Rome on Wednesday, but experience shows that anything can happen in a world that means 'beyond'.

29 April 2018

⇨ The above information is reprinted with kind permission from *The Guardian*. Please visit www.theguardian.com for further information.

From ticket price rises to costly pies, British football fans are being taken for granted

Supporters play a role in this: when did you ever hear one popping up on a phone-in to call for their club's chairman to keep an eye on the purse strings?

By James Moore

Next month's Wembley FA Cup semi-finals have once again turned the national spotlight on ticket prices and the exploitative relationship between football and its fans.

Supporters of Chelsea, Manchester United, Southampton and Tottenham have accused the sport's governing body of 'opportunistic exploitation of fan loyalty' through the imposition of ticket price rises that they say are 'ten times the rate of inflation'.

Prices have been held only for the very cheapest seats, where you can expect the same sort of view as the pigeons circling in the hope of dining out on uneaten chips.

Spurs fans have particular reason to feel aggrieved. Season tickets for the club's brand spanking new stadium in north London went on sale on Monday and some fans face price hikes of up to 70 per cent when compared to what they paid at the decaying, but still much loved, edifice that was the old White Hart Lane.

My interest in the subject was tweaked after colleague Ben Chu wrote on the subject of live music where the existence of a secondary ticketing market (and the scandal over the way it operates) indicates that artists are leaving money on the table.

This is in part because bands thrive through cultivating a relationship with fans. When they play live, they're the organisers of a big party, and the love they get for putting it on could be badly hit were they to be seen to be overly gouging the guests.

Football clubs profit from a similarly unusual, and close, relationship with their supporters. When you buy a ticket for a match, you're signalling your membership of a tribe. You're participating in a shared experience with thousands of like-minded souls.

As with a ticket for a gig, this is not an everyday economic transaction. It's not the same as buying the groceries.

An unhappy Tottenham fan who called into BBC Radio 5 Live's 606 phone-in used the supermarket analogy to highlight the issue created by the price hike he was facing, which called into question whether he'd be able to afford to experience the much loved tradition of taking the kids to the big game.

He pointed out that if he were unhappy with Sainsbury's prices he could go to Tesco. A very different dynamic is at work with a football club: Spurs fans would rather cut off their own legs than switch to, say, West Ham, in protest at prices at their new stadium. If you were to suggest it to them, it probably wouldn't go well for you.

The pushback against high prices in the wake of fan protests, and MPs scenting a handy bandwagon to jump on, has had some success in keeping charges down.

The BBC's annual price of football study revealed that across the board more than 80 per cent of ticket prices in the Premier League were either reduced or frozen for the 2017–18 season. Average season ticket prices fell for the second consecutive year.

Part of the reason is TV. The revenues from the huge contracts the Premiership has been securing for its broadcast rights long ago eclipsed those derived from match day ticket sales.

But having full stadiums is important to the TV companies that shell out their billions. The sound and fury of the crowd is a hugely important part of a TV product that is sold not just domestically, but internationally.

The presence of a healthy number of away fans is of particular value. While they make up a relatively small proportion of most crowds, they often make the most noise through the real hardcore devotees being clustered together. TV viewers are drawn in by the atmosphere they create.

The Premier League's introduction of a £30 cap on the price away fans pay for tickets was therefore not only good PR. It made economic sense at a time of increasing resistance among fans to what they were being asked to pay to get into grounds on top of the expense in terms of time and travel they were investing.

Some clubs, particularly the smaller ones, have paid attention to their fans' economic circumstances when it comes to home games too, and to the value of cultivating a mutually beneficial relationship with them, particularly in the case of families. Huddersfield with its £100 season ticket Premier Plan is a good example.

Other clubs have also run offers, although it should be noted that even after the recent price freeze, fans in the UK pay far in excess of their continental peers, to the extent that it would be cost effective for some to hop on Ryanair or EasyJet flights to join them.

The instinct to squeeze the British football fan remains strong. If it's not through tickets, as with the FA and Spurs, then it's through the price of pies or other ancillary products.

Fans play a role in this. When did you ever hear one popping up on a phone-in to call for their club's chairman to keep an eye on the purse strings and not meet the star player's wage demands.

With fancy stadia to meet repayments on (as in the case of Tottenham), plus the cost of buying players and paying their appalling salaries, many clubs will continue to ask why they should leave a single penny on the table when the fans appear willing to pay up, even if they're not happy about it.

Clubs charge what they charge because they can.

The notion of cultivating a long-term relationship with families? There's nothing like winning to bring 'em in.

That attitude among some clubs will continue to exist until fans do more than hold banners up at grounds.

They only thing that will force a reassessment is if they vote with their feet and with their wallets. There isn't much sign of that happening among the current generation. It might be different with the next one.

24 March 2018

⇨ The above information is reprinted with kind permission from *The Independent*. Please visit www.independent.co.uk for further information.

Bridge fans breathe a sigh of relief: bridge is now a sport

By Peter Stockdale, Communications Officer for the English Bridge Union

The English Bridge Union is delighted at the recommendation from the Advocate General at the European Court, that 'mind sports', and specifically Bridge, should be given equal standing to 'more physical' sports when relating to VAT. The EU's VAT exemption for sport supports competitive activities which have benefits for the health and well-being of the participant. Most people likely approve of the sentiment of the regulation, but arguments over any individual's definition of 'sport' detracts from the point that encouraging and enabling more people to play Bridge should also be encouraged. First and foremost, Bridge is played for fun. Ask anyone who plays, and they will say they do so because they enjoy it. Dig deeper and you reveal why the public should support any measure which enables more people to play.

Brain game Bridge is mentally challenging. Most participants love the fact that their little grey cells get a work-out. Remembering which cards have been played, and working out how to best play the remaining cards – every hand is different and presents a new problem which must be solved. The court's ruling recognised the mental effort and training required, and the positive effect which this has on the health and well-being of the participant. Research has shown that the mental processes involved in playing Bridge can be beneficial to a child's maths skills, and that mind sports can assist in delaying the onset of cognitive decline in older people. These benefits can be enjoyed by everyone, as you can play Bridge to whatever level you choose. Bridge is played for fun, and the positive side effects of challenging yourself mentally are just a bonus. It is also a partnership game. You and your partner must work together to beat your opponents. This social interaction is what sets Bridge apart from other pursuits which may be mentally taxing, but are undertaken alone, or at home.

At a time when social isolation amongst the elderly is an increasing problem, Bridge offers a way for them to interact with others, whilst engaging in their favourite pastime. Playing Bridge fosters many of the same qualities as a 'physical sport' – using teamwork, practising hard, playing by the rules, winning and losing with dignity – and offers a way to compete. For young people who aren't good at team sports, or older people who can no longer play cricket or football, it is important for them to learn or use these skills, and to be competitive. Bridge is the ideal way for them to do this. The inclusion of 'mind sports' within the definition of 'sport' should not be seen as detracting from the benefits of raising your heart rate. It instead should be seen as a progressive move to recognise that there are more activities which should be supported and promoted for the benefit of the health and well-being of the public, and that mind sports meet this objective. The two types of sport can co-exist within the same piece of legislation, and we are delighted that the EU court looks set to agree.

16 June 2017

⇨ The above information is reprinted with kind permission from iNews. Please visit www.inews.co.uk for further information.

Do the Olympics still matter?

With all the ethical and political problems facing the Olympics, do they still matter?
An article from **The Conversation.**

THE C⊙NVERSATION

By Bruce Kidd, Vice-President and Principal, University of Toronto

As someone who proudly wears his Olympic heart on his sleeve – I competed in the 1964 Games in Tokyo and have been involved in a variety of roles ever since – I get asked that question all the time, especially when another Games approach. And my answer is still in the affirmative.

While circumstances change, and I'd like to think I make a fresh calculation each time, I still believe the Olympics contribute a net benefit to humanity. I'm excited about the forthcoming Winter Olympic and Winter Paralympic Games in Pyeongchang, South Korea.

For those of us who pursue and watch sports, it's the only forum where the entire world gets to compete on a multi-sport basis. While it's the polar countries that excel, the Winter Olympics and Paralympics will attract competitors from an estimated 90 national communities, representing more than two-thirds of the world's population.

In an increasingly privatised sports place, with a hardening monoculture of fewer and fewer sports and competitors, the Olympics provide the greatest range of national and regional accessibility.

Provides support, visibility

For Canadians, it's the primary place where athletes in the rarely publicised but culturally important sports of skiing, skating, luge, skeleton and bobsled have recognised opportunities – and with few exceptions, the only time Canadian women and para-athletes get any significant support and visibility.

If it wasn't for the Olympics to stimulate government investment in women's and para sports and the worldwide coverage to attract advertisers, women and para-athletes would be even more underfunded and invisible in mainstream sports coverage than they are now.

So for those who believe in an equitable, broadly based and accessible sports system, the Olympics provide a very important incentive – and even legitimisation.

It's also fantastic sport, and gives us a chance to see remarkable athletes from all across Canada go up against the best from other countries, and represent Canada to the world. I'll be glued to my television.

What's more, the Olympics make a genuine effort to affirm and encourage humanitarian international and intercultural education and exchange – no mean contribution in this increasingly war-torn, nativist and xenophobic world.

Bringing people together

In my long experience, this is real and sets the tone for the millions of sporting exchanges between people of widely different backgrounds that occur around the world throughout the year.

The joint North and South Korean team that will march and compete together in Pyeongchang, and the resumption of communication that it has initiated, is just one example where the Olympics and international sport have brought bitterly divided people into the same room for peaceful exchange.

The Olympics contribute significantly to the development of sports around the world, especially among the poorest countries, distributing a big share of its television revenue – US$509 million from 2017–20.

One priority is sport for refugees. The very first Refugee Olympic Team, made up of athletes from refugee camps in four different countries, competed in Rio in 2016. Many Olympic athletes, such as Canada's Rosie MacLennan, have been inspired by their experiences to contribute to sport for development across the Global South.

To be sure, the Olympics face a host of daunting challenges, including the ginormous costs of staging games, corruption in governance, human rights abuses and doping.

The issues are so formidable that fewer and fewer cities are interested in hosting them, and in some liberal-democratic countries, voters have turned back bids. It remains to be seen whether Calgary will actually go ahead with plans to bid for the 2026 Winter Olympics and Paralympics.

Addressing many challenges

But I would also say the Olympic leadership is preoccupied with addressing these challenges. One solution to rising costs is to use existing facilities as much as possible, spread out new facilities, placing them where they are most needed as Toronto did for the 2015 Pan American and Parapan American Games, and reduce seating for spectators, recognising that most of the world watches on television. The Olympics vigorously tries to prevent and punish doping, as the current spat with Russia readily indicates.

While the Olympics have introduced important reforms in recent years, including transparent financial accounting and an affirmation against discrimination based on an athlete's sexual orientation, it's not easy to introduce and implement progressive change in a way that keeps the entire world together.

I am enraged by the Russians' state-directed doping in Sochi and support Canadian Olympic leaders who call for them to be banned from Pyeongchang. Yet I have European friends who fear Russian isolation and applaud IOC president Thomas Bach's diplomatic gymnastics to balance sanctions and representation.

A big-tent approach requires a low threshold if you want everyone there. If we only competed with countries that shared our values, we would have very few competitors indeed. But it makes the world of Olympic sports very difficult to govern.

I'm quite happy if people continue to be critical of Olympic practices or blind spots – I'm critical of some of them too – but to give up on the project because the international sports world is not perfect would be really short-sighted. It would also deny Canadians an opportunity to participate in, and contribute to, a humanitarian movement that's still very important.

4 February 2018

⇨ The above information is reprinted with kind permission from *The Conversation*. Please visit www.theconversation.com for further information.

© 2010-2018, The Conversation Trust (UK)

Physical activity guidelines for children and young people

How much physical activity should children and young people aged five to 18 do to keep healthy?

To stay healthy or to improve health, young people need to do three types of physical activity each week:

⇨ aerobic exercise

⇨ exercises to strengthen their bones

⇨ exercises to strengthen their muscles.

The amount of physical activity you need to do each week is determined by your age.

⇨ early childhood (under five years old)

⇨ adults (19 to 64 years old)

⇨ older adults (65 and over)

Guidelines for five- to 18-year-olds

To maintain a basic level of health, children and young people aged five to 18 need to do:

⇨ at least 60 minutes of physical activity every day – this should range from moderate activity, such as cycling and playground activities, to vigorous activity, such as running and tennis

⇨ on three days a week, these activities should involve exercises for strong muscles and bones, such as swinging on playground equipment, hopping and skipping, and sports such as gymnastics or tennis.

Children and young people should also reduce the time they spend sitting for extended periods of time, including watching TV, playing computer games and travelling by car when they could walk or cycle.

Being active for at least 60 minutes a day is linked to better general health, stronger bones and muscles, and higher levels of self-esteem.

What counts as moderate activity?

Examples of activities that require moderate effort for most young people include:

⇨ walking to school

⇨ playing in the playground

⇨ riding a scooter

⇨ skateboarding

⇨ rollerblading

⇨ walking the dog

⇨ cycling on level ground or ground with few hills.

Moderate activity raises your heart rate and makes you sweat. One way to tell if your activity is moderate is if you can still talk but cannot sing the words to a song.

What counts as vigorous activity?

There is good evidence vigorous activity can bring health benefits over and above that of moderate activity. A rule of thumb is that one minute of vigorous activity provides the same health benefits as two minutes of moderate activity.

There's currently no recommendation on how long a session of vigorous activity should be for this age group.

Examples of activities that require vigorous effort for most young people include:

⇨ playing chase

⇨ energetic dancing

⇨ swimming

- ⇨ running
- ⇨ gymnastics
- ⇨ football
- ⇨ rugby
- ⇨ martial arts, such as karate
- ⇨ cycling fast or on hilly terrain.

Vigorous activity makes you breathe hard and fast. If your activity is vigorous, you won't be able to say more than a few words without pausing for a breath.

What activities strengthen muscles?

Muscle strength is necessary for daily activities, and to build and maintain strong bones, regulate blood sugar and blood pressure, and help maintain a healthy weight.

For young people, muscle-strengthening activities are those that require them to lift their own body weight or work against a resistance, such as lifting a weight.

Examples of muscle-strengthening activities suitable for children include:

- ⇨ games such as tug of war
- ⇨ swinging on playground equipment bars
- ⇨ gymnastics
- ⇨ rope or tree climbing
- ⇨ sit-ups, press-ups and other similar exercises
- ⇨ gymnastics
- ⇨ football
- ⇨ rugby
- ⇨ tennis.

Examples of muscle-strengthening activities suitable for young people include:

- ⇨ sit-ups, press-ups and other similar exercises

- ⇨ gymnastics
- ⇨ resistance exercises with exercise bands, weight machines or handheld weights
- ⇨ rock climbing
- ⇨ football
- ⇨ basketball
- ⇨ tennis

Children and young people should take part in activities appropriate for their age and stage of development.

What activities strengthen bones?

Examples of bone-strengthening activities for children include:

- ⇨ activities that require children to lift their body weight or work against a resistance
- ⇨ jumping and climbing activities, combined with the use of playground equipment and toys
- ⇨ games such as hopscotch
- ⇨ skipping with a rope
- ⇨ walking
- ⇨ running
- ⇨ gymnastics
- ⇨ dance
- ⇨ football

- ⇨ basketball
- ⇨ martial arts

Examples of bone-strengthening activities for young people include:

- ⇨ dance
- ⇨ aerobics
- ⇨ weight training
- ⇨ running
- ⇨ gymnastics
- ⇨ football
- ⇨ rugby
- ⇨ netball
- ⇨ hockey
- ⇨ badminton
- ⇨ tennis
- ⇨ skipping with a rope
- ⇨ martial arts.

Children and young people should take part in activities appropriate for their age and stage of development.

25 June 2018

- ⇨ The above information is reproduced with kind permission from the NHS. Please visit www.nhs.uk for further information

Women and sport

Sing when you're women: why it's time to take female sports fans seriously

An article from The Conversation.

THE CONVERSATION

By Stacey Pope, Associate Professor in School of Applied Social Sciences, Durham University

When it comes to sports, die-hard fans are often thought of as the men in the crowd. But my new research shows, that despite popular stereotypes of women lacking sporting knowledge or only being interested in the sexual attractiveness of (male) star players – female fans are just as passionate and committed to their clubs as the men.

Based on a host of intensive interviews with football and rugby union fans from three generations in one area in the UK (Leicester), my latest findings show that, unlike the stereotypes, sport plays a hugely important role in the lives and identities of many female fans.

Perhaps in part because of these popular (and sexist) assumptions and stereotypes of female fans, very little research has examined women's experiences as sports fans. Most studies have instead focused exclusively on male supporters and issues of fan rivalry and hooliganism.

My work tackles head-on the lack of research on female sports fans. It also challenges the perceptions of women as inauthentic or inferior fans in comparison to male supporters.

The female fan

My own research shows there is a huge diversity of female supporter styles – meaning that there is a need to move away from distinctions between males as 'authentic' and 'real' supporters and

females as 'inauthentic' or not 'real' fans.

What came through the research was two fan types: dedicated or highly committed 'hot' fans, and more casual 'cool' fans. Nearly 85% of the football fans and just under half of the rugby union fans I spoke to could best be described as 'hot' sports fans.

For these dedicated fans, sport was an important aspect of their identity. This was often illustrated with mentions of their team on their CV, or by making new people they meet aware they are a fan of a particular club. These female fans invested large amounts of time watching or thinking about sport, with some of the extreme fans confessing that their club or team is almost 'constantly' on their mind – as one female football fan explained:

'Football's always been my life. Like I

said, playing it, watching it … I like lots of different sports but football's always been the one if you like … the love of my life. That's me, that's part of me.'

For female rugby union fans it was the same. One season ticket holder told me about the role sport plays in her life:

'In order of priority, it's (Leicester) Tigers and then it's my other half and then it's the kids and the grand-kids, you know, and everybody, they all know it. They've been told that that's the order of importance.'

The highs and lows

For these fans, sport produces extremes in terms of emotional responses depending on the match-day results – and invariably this then impacts on relations with close relatives. For example, because the club formed such a significant part of these fan's lives, organising other activities became extremely complicated – with some describing how family weddings needed to be planned carefully not to coincide with football matches.

Some of the intense football fans also confessed that they could not enter into a relationship with a supporter who did not follow the same club. As one female fan put it:

'It's a big part of my life, and if he can't accept me as a Leicester fan then I'm afraid I don't want to know you, sort of thing.'

Many fans also reported having rooms or even a home dressed in club colours and products. And some of the football women also reported having tattoos of the club to demonstrate their allegiance.

A man's world?

For the smaller number of 'cool' female fans, the research showed sport did not impact upon their lives in the same way. Sport was viewed more as a 'hobby' or form of 'entertainment' – a leisure choice or 'just one of the things I do in my spare time'.

While some female fans were fairly rooted as either 'hot' or 'cool' female fans, in some cases there was some shifting between these two modes. Having children was shown to be one of the main factors which affected this movement – which is probably representative of the fact that many women are still responsible for the main bulk of childcare and housework.

What all this shows is the need to start taking female sports fans more seriously. Because by dismissing women who love their club as much as they love their family, not only are a large number of the fan base being alienated, but ultimately there is also a risk of sport becoming a male-only pastime.

14 July 2017

⇨ The above information is reprinted with kind permission from *The Conversation*. Please visit www.theconversation.com for further information.

40 per cent of women in sport industry face gender discrimination, report finds

Women in Sport is on a mission to create a 'more inclusive workplace culture'.

By Sabrina Barr

A new report conducted by Women in Sport has revealed that 40 per cent of women experience gender discrimination in the sport industry.

The report, titled *Beyond 30 per cent – Workplace Culture in Sport*, has unveiled the extent to which women with careers in sport experience prejudice.

A survey of 1,152 women and men working in sport was conducted between September 2017 and March 2018 as part of the study, with 42 in-depth interviews carried out with some of the participants.

38 per cent of the women stated that they've experienced gender discrimination in the workplace, in comparison to a fifth of the men.

Moreover, 40 per cent of the women felt that their gender can have a negative impact on the way in which they're valued by others at work, while 30 per cent have experienced inappropriate behaviour from someone of the opposite sex in comparison to a tenth of the men.

When asked whether men and women in their workplace are treated equally and fairly, 72 per cent of the men believed that they were.

However, when asked the same question, only 46 per cent of women agreed.

Women in Sport hopes that its report can spur an increase in the number of women attaining positions of leadership in sport, in addition to addressing the stark sexism that's rife throughout the industry.

'Women in Sport is committed to ensuring sport develops, and benefits from, equality,' said Ruth Holdaway, CEO of Women in Sport.

'By shining a light on gender discrimination in the sport workplace we are raising awareness of specific problems so that we can work together with the sector to create positive change.'

She continued, stating that although there have been efforts to solve gender discrimination within sport, much more needs to be done.

'We led this research to provide the sport sector with in-depth understanding of the issues that affect women in the sport workplace,' she said.

'Now we want to work with sports organisations to build a more inclusive workplace culture, where both women and men can reach their full potential.'

According to the report, less than half of the National Governing Bodies of sport have succeeded in achieving the minimum requirement of 30 per cent of women on the board.

20 June 2018

⇨ The above information is reprinted with kind permission from *The Independent*. Please visit www.independent.co.uk for further information.

Sport participation in England

By Lukas Audickas

Key points (England)

More men than women participate in sport

Around 63% of men were active in sport compared to 58% of women, based on the Active Lives Survey data for year ending May 2017.

Women prefer walking for leisure, men general sports

The most popular physical activity among women was walking for leisure (24%) followed by fitness activities (19%) in May 2017. Men were the most active in general sporting activities (29% of men compared to just under 17% of women).

Around 43% of people with a disability were active in sport

On average 43% of people with a disability participated in sport activities for over 150 minutes a week in year ending May 2017. This was more than 20 percentage points lower than 65% of those with no disability.

Highest participation among highest social classes

Around 70% of individuals in managerial, administrative and professional occupations were active in sport in year ending May 2017. In contrast, around 49% of those long term unemployed or never worked were active in sport.

Running, fitness and gym – popular in 2016/17

In year ending May 2017, the most common activity was running (15%) followed by fitness class (14%) and gym (12%), ranked by proportion of population participating at least twice over the last 28 days prior to survey.

South West region was the most active in 2016/17

Participation in sport was highest in South West region (around 63%) and lowest in West Midlands (53%), compared to 61% in England overall. The proportion of people who were fairly active was similar across all regions in England – at around 14%.

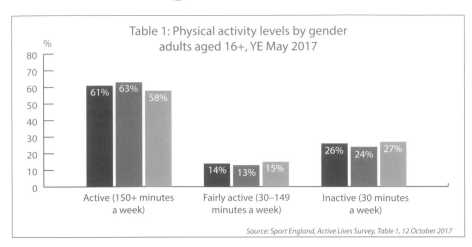

Table 1: Physical activity levels by gender adults aged 16+, YE May 2017

Source: Sport England, Active Lives Survey, Table 1, 12 October 2017

UK had the second highest rate of sport workers in the EU

The UK had the second highest rate of 659 sport workers per 100,000 population, compared to other EU countries in 2016. Sweden was the first with 757 and Denmark was third with 569. UK rate in 2016 was twice as high as the EU 28 average of 332.

Gender

Table 1 above indicates that 63% of men were active in sport compared to 58% of women, based on the Active Lives Survey data for year ending May 2017.

Between 2005/06 and 2015/16, around 10% more men than women participated in sport activities, according to Active People Survey data.

There was a statistically significant increase of over one percentage point participation in 2015/16 compared to 2005/06.

Gender and broad activity types

Table 2 shows that the most popular physical activity among women was walking for leisure (24%) followed by fitness activities (19%) and walking for travel (18%) in May 2017. Men were the most active in general sporting activities* (29% of men compared to just under 17% of women). The least common activity across both genders was creative or artistic dancing. Just around 1% of men and 2% of women participated in creative dancing in year ending May 2017.

14 December 2017

⇨ The above information is reprinted with kind permission from House of Commons Library. Please visit www.parliament.uk for further information.

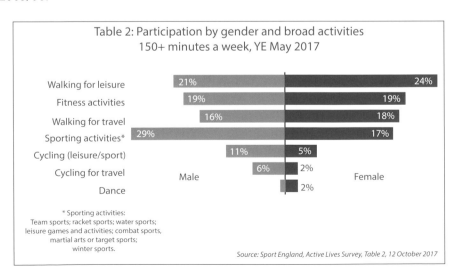

Table 2: Participation by gender and broad activities 150+ minutes a week, YE May 2017

	Male	Female
Walking for leisure	21%	24%
Fitness activities	19%	19%
Walking for travel	16%	18%
Sporting activities*	29%	17%
Cycling (leisure/sport)	11%	5%
Cycling for travel	6%	2%
Dance		2%

* Sporting activities: Team sports; racket sports; water sports; leisure games and activities; combat sports, martial arts or target sports; winter sports.

Source: Sport England, Active Lives Survey, Table 2, 12 October 2017

Boosting the profile of women's sports

Telegraph *columnist Jim White talks to rugby star and pundit Maggie Alphonsi MBE about her career and the rise of women's sports.*

On Thursday 15 March, senior executives from the sports industry gathered for an exclusive interview with rugby star and pundit Maggie Alphonsi MBE, conducted by *Telegraph* columnist Jim White, covering her career as a player and broadcaster, as well as her experience of the rise of women's sports.

The discussion provided fascinating insights and advice which can apply to all sports:

Making the game accessible to all backgrounds

Having grown up in an area where rugby was unheard of for both boys and girls, Maggie knows what it takes to improve diversity and inclusivity of the sport. She plans to promote the uptake of rugby across the board by growing the women's game. When women's teams succeed, we see the knock-on effect and increased popularity of sport amongst girls and boys across the country, whether in hockey, cricket or rugby.

Social media as a tool for self-promotion despite a lack of media coverage

Social media has been key for the promotion of women's rugby because the women's game is in need of greater media coverage. Direct access to audiences lets players promote the women's game themselves, whilst maintaining that all-important human element and revealing their true personalities.

How strategic fixture scheduling can boost audiences

Scheduling women's matches immediately before or after the men's might lead to greater exposure with audiences catching kick off or the tailend of the former. However, add-on scheduling completely overlooks the excitement of the women's game in its own right. Instead, joint scheduling with under-20s has boosted audience numbers and looks set to create a buzz similar to France, where venues compete for the right to host women's games.

29 March 2018

⇨ The above information is reprinted with kind permission from *The Telegraph*. Please visit www.telegraph.co.uk for further information.

Gender pay gap in sport is justified – women's games can't come close to matching the men's earning power

By Ewan MacKenna

In November of 2016, a story on the CBS show *60 minutes* began a broader debate across the sporting spectrum.

That night, World Cup winners Carli Lloyd, Becky Sauerbrunn, Morgan Brian and Christen Press solemnly talked about a case they were taking against their governing body in relation to unequal pay versus their counterparts on the US men's national team.

They even suggested they should get more as 'we win, we're successful, we should get what we deserve'.

'This is about gender discrimination,' added Press, 'and I don't think that positive change occurs in the world unless it has to.'

She was right in the assertion made in the second part of that statement. She was merely presumed to be right around the first part.

With so much justified tarring of and outrage towards a male-dominated-and-dictated society, there's a trend that's bravely trying to bring about discussion and change in regards to discrimination in employment. Still nascent, but vitally shining a light, just this week the respected journalist Carrie Grace quit from her role as BBC's China Editor in protest at the organisation's attitude to the same reward for the same work, while in Iceland a new equal-pay law had to be introduced.

From those US women onwards, sport became a part of that fight, and in recent weeks it's carried on with Australia's rugby players and Norway's soccer players reaching pay parity.

You can expect the calls to grow further and wider and louder. Here for instance, we've had 46,286 at the last women's All Ireland final; we've had our own women's soccer team taking a stand; we've had the island host the women's Rugby World Cup which was quickly branded a success. But stop there, for so much of women's sport is patronised with politically correct misinformation rather than scrutinised. The truth is sport can never reach parity nor should it be forced to.

Look at it another way. While a big crowd at a women's football final is something to be proud of, how many care the rest of the year when bus loads with free tickets don't make their way to the deciding game? A decent interest at the UCD bowl for women's rugby is important too but ever ask why the opening game for the hosts wasn't in Lansdowne Road?

As for the women's soccer team, how many praised them, but wouldn't go to see them, or could even name any of them? The wider interest is not there. That's not sexist but what is sexist is

Bums on seats-based payment

to lie to female sportspeople about what their triumphs and disasters mean to the masses, based purely on their gender.

A key statistic used on that *60 Minutes* broadcast back in 2016 and in the debate that followed was that the biggest ever US TV audience for a soccer game had tuned into the women's 2015 crowning glory. But comparing US men's and women's friendlies before their last respective World Cups, 70 per cent more tuned in to the men; comparing send-off games, that number was 87 per cent greater; in group games at those two tournaments, 212 per cent more watched the men.

Even when you include that record 25 million who turned on the 2015 final, the US men outdrew the US women by 74 per cent as an average across all World Cup games. On top of that, while broadcaster Fox brought in $17 million in ad revenue from women's games in 2015, ESPN brought in $529 million from the last men's tournament. That's all this really comes down to.

Still, others tried and try to follow suit. Highlighting their own success, last year the US women's ice hockey side initially said they'd refuse to defend their title because of pay disparity, but compare the two world championships. Hosting the tournament they finally agreed to play in, that women's team brought in an average of under 2,500 fans across their handful of games while away in Germany the men got more than 14,000 per game. We could go on. As for example in women's tennis, BT had next to no competition for the rights while for the men, Amazon just forked out a fortune. The former is consistently struggling to move tickets too.

Don't confuse all this for what it's not however. Sure enough the promotion and appointment of women into administration roles, into coaching roles, and into media roles is way behind where it should be and needs to be. Meanwhile, when it comes to grassroots sport and kids sport, where participation and enjoyment rather than business is the driver, of course the pie should be split down the middle. But when it gets to an elite level, then it's something different,

for that is when it becomes about capitalism. Thus if women in high-end sport want to look for a pay rise, that's their right, but using gender equality as some sort of leverage is both cynical and it's wrong.

Competing in a different arena against different opponents for different prizes doesn't constitute equal work. If we were to go down that path, should a League of Ireland player not earn the same as a La Liga player? Imagine the laughter if they tried to even put forward a case. Instead, when the day comes that they bring in the same money, then let them earn the same money.

Yet in the face of this the disparity in remuneration is thrown out annually as if to disturb a reflex reaction. A couple of years back when Wayne Rooney was earning £300,000 a week and was his country's best-paid player, he was compared to Steph Houghton who was on £1,200. At the men's US Open in golf the winner's cheque is $2.16 million, two-and-a-half times as much as the women's winner takes home. In cricket, their men's World Cup winners get more by a multiple of seven. And in the latest ranking of the 100 highest-paid athletes, there is only one woman on the list at 51. It goes on.

The highest-paid player in the WNBA makes roughly one-fifth of the lowest-paid player in NBA. But so what? Are all these figures supposed to make us feign outrage? There's a good reason. On that last stat, remember the NBA brings in over $5 billion – with Turner Sports and ESPN paying a combined $2.6 billionn annually – while ESPN's annual commitment to the WNBA is $12 million. It means these wages aren't based around gender but on earning power and that earning power is based on what people want to see.

You can't force the public to care. Name the fastest woman in the world? Name the women's number one tennis player? Name the Dublin female captain? We bet most can't and that's fine, but as an extension pay is set by demand and not by fairness, and fans make paydays possible with the popularity of the sport almost always linked intrinsically to the amount athletes are paid.

Ultimately better athleticism tends to result in sport being played at a faster, higher, stronger level and that's what most want.

Plain and simple, women are relatively slower, lower, weaker. Last year the same US women's side that wanted equal pay lost a game to the FC Dallas under-15 boys academy 5-2, while a year prior to that, as they prepared for an Olympics where they'd be a penalty shoot-out away from a medal game, Australia's national women's team suffered a 7-0 loss to the Newcastle Jets under-15 boys side. There's no shame or surprise in any of that for, as a starting point, it's just science and biology. Throw in incentives and expertise created and demanded by the big business and mass markets of men's sport, and it means the gap will grow and grow.

It may not seem right, and it's sure not fair, but that doesn't stop it being true.

Last year Sharon Hutchinson, former Irish international hockey goalkeeper and the founder of the excellent sportswomen.ie, noted: 'I think women's sport has been taken more seriously rather than just "ah sure, aren't they great". I do think it's definitely changed and we can now be critical of women's sport too, just as we do with men's sport so, if they're not playing well, we can say they're not playing well and that is a big change.' Such fair criticism ought to continue into undeserved and unfair attempts to balance wages as well.

What's crucial is not to conflate pay in sport with the pay revolution elsewhere, for it hijacks and takes away from what women in other industries are standing up for. Here though it's simply looking for the same when you bring in less. That is the definition of inequality, a concept we are desperately trying to escape.

11 January 2018

⇨ The above information is reprinted with kind permission from *The Independent*. Please visit www.independent.ie for further information.

This Girl Can returns to our screens

Nationwide campaign to get women and girls moving, regardless of shape, size and ability, returns to inspire more women.

The new advert – which launched online in February 2017, and hit television screens during the ad break of *Coronation Street* – saw a range of new and returning faces, new messages and hard-hitting mantras to prompt a change in attitudes and help boost women's confidence.

Staying true to its original formula of showing real women and girls playing sport and getting active, the message is clear: it's OK to sweat, it's OK to jiggle, it's OK not to be brilliant (or to be brilliant) and it's normal for life to get in the way sometimes.

Our ambition is still about empowering women and breaking down the barriers that are stopping women and girls getting active – and we're now widening our scope to target women aged from 14 up to 60 and beyond.

New artwork and phrases for the second wave of the campaign, including 'Unleash your inner beginner', 'A kick right in the stereotypes' and 'Take me as I am or watch me as I go', have been splashed across billboards and shopping centres up and down the country in recent weeks.

I'm a woman, phenomenally

The mantras speak directly to fears and worries women have surrounding sport and physical activity, such as not being good enough, or overcoming stereotypes about what women should or shouldn't do.

The second wave responds to what we've learned about what does and doesn't motivate women to get involved in physical activity since the original campaign launched two years ago.

We'll be showing women that it doesn't matter if you become active, stop, and then start again or do something different – it's a normal process and a part of life.

Set to a new soundtrack by Beth Ditto blended with a narrative by the iconic poet, Maya Angelou, the new advert sees familiar faces from the original advert, Grace and Alice, return and continue their story.

Some of the other personal stories brought to life in the film include new mum Stephanie Outlaw, 69-year-old outdoor swimmer Sue Bairstow, student kickboxer Fakhira Mohamad Hassan Mukhtar and blade-runner Debbie Squance from Plymouth, who all show the ways they overcome the worries that can hold women back.

Jennie Price, Sport England chief executive, said: 'This Girl Can has made a real difference since it launched, with the number of women doing regular physical activity and sport now at an all-time high. But there's a lot more to do.

'Our research showed the dialogue many of us have in our heads about whether we look OK, whether we are good enough, whether we belong here doesn't go away – we just learn to manage it.

'A new message this time is something women don't usually hear: it's OK to take a break, to have a week off, to walk not run. Nobody is saying this to us.

'Many of the women we've featured talk about stopping, then starting again. It can feel like the hardest thing in the world to return after a few weeks off, when you fear you've lost ground or fitness, but we want to surface this as a discussion point, to say it's normal to take a break, but that needn't stop you for good.''

Changing behaviour

This Girl Can was the first campaign of its kind to celebrate women of all shapes, sizes and levels of ability getting active in all their sweaty, jiggly glory.

The results have been remarkable since the first wave at the start of 2015.

> # 2.8 million
> **women more active thanks to This Girl Can**

The original campaign received over 95 million views and 733,000 mentions across social media. The campaign created a very large and active social community, with 581,000 followers across all platforms and over 1.2 million visits to the website.

Most importantly, This Girl Can is changing behaviour.

More women and girls are now active as a result of This Girl Can – 2.8 million women have been more active as a result of seeing the campaign. The number of women playing sport and getting active once a week, every week, has also increased by 250,000 since we launched the campaign.

This Girl Can is funded thanks to Lottery players and Arabella Gilchrist, head of brand for The National Lottery, said: 'We're incredibly proud of our association with This Girl Can and especially the impact it has had on British women over the past 12 months – to be able to say that funds raised by National Lottery players are enabling the next phase fills us with immense pride.'

24 February 2017

⇨ The above information is reprinted with kind permission from Sport England. Please visit www.sportengland.org for further information.

© 2018 Sport England

Forbes' rich list shows sport fails to respect women – let alone pay them properly

Until women are respected in the same way men are, such lists and the gender pay gap will not shift.

By Kate O'Halloran

Forbes has released its list of the top 100 paid athletes in the world with one glaring omission: not a single woman made the list. This is the first time this has happened since the list was expanded to at least 50 people in 2010. While perhaps unsurprising to some, this stark reality is a reminder of how far sport has to go when it comes to gender equity – and perhaps more important, it suggests that things are getting worse.

The gender pay gap in sport is well known. Figures from the Sporting Intelligence annual salary survey in November 2017 found that gender inequality is more entrenched in sport than in politics, business, medicine and space exploration. Included in the report was the astonishing fact that the Paris Saint-Germain and Brazil forward Neymar, who ranked fifth on *Forbes*' 2018 list, was paid more than the entire top seven women's football leagues combined.

Take a moment for that to sink in: in what kind of world do we value a single men's football player more than seven leagues of women?

The 2018 *Forbes* list is even more startling when you take in the mammoth figures men's sport stars are paid. Lionel Messi, who comes in second, was paid $111 million, with $84 million in salary or winnings and a further $27 million in endorsements. Just one per cent of Messi's salary equates to $1.1 million. Just how many women's sport stars are paid that much, worldwide? The list is probably shorter than the 100 men listed by *Forbes*.

Perhaps the most disturbing thing about this list is the name at the top: boxer Floyd Mayweather. Mayweather has been convicted of violence against women: twice having pleaded guilty, once having been convicted only to have those charges dismissed five years later, and once having been sentenced to 90 days in jail (only to be released after 60 days) for hitting the mother of his children, in front of them. However, he was never suspended by the Nevada boxing commission after pleading guilty – and now earns a cool $285 million, with $275 million in salary and winnings and $10 million in endorsements.

If you consider that Mayweather is the world's highest-paid athlete, and that not a single woman makes the list, a couple of clear messages emerge: first, there aren't sufficient consequences for men who perpetrate violence against women (especially in sport), and second, women simply aren't respected in the same way men are. Until they are, lists like these, or the notorious gender pay gap, currently at 15.3% in Australia, won't shift.

Take for example Serena Williams. Reports on the *Forbes* list have pointed out that Williams was on last year's list – albeit as the sole woman. The reason Williams dropped off the list this year was because she was pregnant. According to Australia's Workplace Gender Equality Agency, two of the key reasons the gender pay gap exists are: women's disproportionate share of unpaid caring and domestic work, and women's greater time out of the workforce, impacting on career progression and opportunities.

Although Williams is an exceptional case, who was incredibly well off during pregnancy (still earning an estimated $18 million off the court in endorsements), she lost nearly $8 million in prize money as a consequence of having her daughter. Clearly, even the most well off aren't immune from the gender pay gap that persists in so many workplaces, sport included.

Perhaps, in some ways, it is useful that Williams didn't make the top 100 this year. Having been the sole woman to make the top 100 in the year before (and one of only two – with her rival Maria Sharapova – in the year before that), her exceptionalism has masked deep inequity for many women across the board, not just at the elite level, and not just in tennis, which persists in being the most lucrative sport for women.

The composition of lists like these must change, but before that can happen, we must start by addressing what underpins gender inequity in sport: respect for women.

6 June 2018

⇨ The above information is reprinted with kind permission from *The Guardian*. Please visit www.theguardian.com for further information.

Female sports fans are breaking down social barriers but still face physical obstacles to their enjoyment of going to a game

An article from the Economic and Social Research Council.

ESRC is part of UK Research and Innovation.

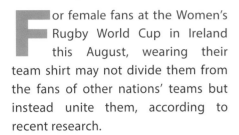

For female fans at the Women's Rugby World Cup in Ireland this August, wearing their team shirt may not divide them from the fans of other nations' teams but instead unite them, according to recent research.

In her book *The Feminization of Sports Fandom*, which is supported by the Economic and Social Research Council, Stacey Pope sheds new light on the ways in which women become sports fans and explores how they negotiate their place in this male domain.

Dr Pope, Associate Professor at Durham University, found that the wearing of a club shirt can not only help female sport supporters to establish and reinforce their identity as fans, but it can also help to generate a collective sense of belonging with other female (and male) supporters.

More than half (50/85) of the female football and rugby union fans she interviewed, suggested that sharing an interest in their sport gave people a common bond or connection with a person they had not met before.

She writes: 'For many female fans, this shared sporting interest or connection could act as a social facilitator, thus easily breaking down geographic or cultural barriers and inviting more or less spontaneous social interaction of a type perhaps less favoured by men who wear club shirts.'

One of her interviewees says: 'When we were in New Zealand with the [British] Lions tour … people would be stopping and talking to you on the street and it was great … It is

that whole thing of an international language … It does introduce you to a whole different class of people; definitely starts whole networks of conversations.'

While this community of like-minded female fans may enjoy the camaraderie outside the grounds, Dr Pope discovered that the experience of supporting their teams in the stadium might not be quite so pleasant.

In her book, Dr Pope questions female fans about 'traditional' or older sports grounds. She found that many female fans expressed strong emotional attachments to their club's home stadium and thus valued the tradition and heritage of their clubs. For example, one respondent described the home stadium as 'one of my favourite places in the world … it just is magic when you get in' and terms such as 'electric', 'special' and 'intense' were used to describe the match-day atmosphere.

However, 'almost half (24/51) of football fans and nearly three-quarters (25/34) of rugby supporters across all age groups complained about numbers of women's toilets at old sports grounds and/or the "abysmal" state of those facilities that did exist'.

More recently, many clubs have moved to new stadiums and/or redeveloped old grounds and Dr Pope explores these attempts to make stadiums more female or family friendly to try to encourage more women to attend matches. But some of the female fans

felt that these newer or redeveloped stadiums still did not go far enough to improve the spaces or facilities for women. Some female fans bemoaned the basic facilities that were available and a small number remained disappointed with the continued lack of female toilets available.

Some older female fans felt that 'men's spatial interests had been more widely prioritised in stadiums'. For example, the concrete concourses at a new football stadium were seen as a conventionally 'masculine' space. One respondent says: 'This area you wait in before you actually go up to sit in your seat, you can buy drinks and you can buy eats, but there's actually nowhere to sit at all … So it's the image for the men, isn't it? They like to stand up and drink a pint.'

Dr Pope writes that 'such poor facilities may be tolerated or accepted by many female fans in the space of the sports stadium, but given the recent wider societal changes which have led to greater equality between the sexes in contemporary society, it seems unlikely that women would be as willing to accept these poor facilities on offer in other public spaces such as in the workplace or other leisure arenas'.

Her findings show that while some women critiqued the poor facilities that were on offer for women, others defended these and suggested that more primitive facilities defined the live sports experience, and not necessarily in a negative way. She suggests that this acceptance of poor facilities in the sports stadium can

be attributed in part to the need for women to 'prove' themselves as sports fans.

Dr Pope said: 'Whereas male fans are assumed to be "authentic" or "real" sports fans, women are typically assumed to be "inauthentic" or "not real" fans, with common stereotypes including that they lack sporting knowledge and/or are only interested in the sexual attractiveness of (male) star players. Therefore, women must always balance any gender issues with the need to present themselves as an "authentic" fan. By recognising and accepting that all facilities at live sport are likely to be quite basic, women accept that suffering mildly at live sports events confirms them as an included and committed fan.

'When seeking to introduce policies to address issues of gender inequality, clubs and governing bodies need to be sensitive to how women experience their fandom in a male-dominated world and must constantly balance being a supporter with being a woman. For example, in my research, the vast majority of female fans were against the club introducing policies that were specifically aimed at women and did not want to be seen as female fans. There were concerns that policies that identified female fans could trigger a "backlash" from male supporters or would actually have a detrimental effect on women. Clubs and governing bodies need to have an understanding of these issues when working with female fans to improve their match-day experiences and stadium facilities."

Dr Pope suggested one way that sports clubs and governing bodies could develop more female-friendly and accessible stadiums would be to introduce match-day childcare facilities. Her research findings show that male and female fans may follow different fan careers across their lives, with many women compelled to take 'fan breaks' after having children. Childcare facilities are fairly rare at sports stadia, but this could enhance the experiences of some female fans (and, indeed, the male fans who have childcare responsibilities). Dr Pope added that, in the longer term, this could also have financial incentives for clubs by helping to develop a connection with younger generations.

4 August 2017

⇨ The above information is reprinted with kind permission from the Economic and Social Research Council. Please visit www.esrc. ukri.org for further information.

Britain's Olympic women 'drive surge in sport for teenage girls'

By Padraic Flanagan

Olympic success by Team GB's women has helped trigger a surge in teenage girls taking up sport, according to a new report. Three in four girls aged 15 and 16 are now playing sport at school, compared with only one in two in 2015, say researchers behind the Childwise report into children's behaviour. The dramatic rise is also seen in girls playing sport in their own time, with half of all teenage girls now participating at home and school compared with only two in five two years ago. 'Girls aged 15 and 16 have always been the group least likely to take part in any sport, at school or outside school, but the news that more of them are now doing sport at school is very encouraging,' said Simon Leggett, Research Director from Childwise.

Success

He singled out media campaigns aimed at encouraging girls and women into sport, such as Sport England's 'This Girl Can', and the success of British Olympic stars such as Jessica Ennis-Hill for inspiring the surge. 'This year we may be witnessing the impact of many years of campaigning, along with female success at both the London 2012 and Rio 2016 Olympics,' said Mr Leggett. Netball is the most popular sport at school for girls aged 11 to 16, with 57 per cent of all girls playing, followed by athletics at 45 per cent, badminton at 39 per cent and hockey at 35 per cent. Outside school, swimming is most popular followed by cycling and athletics.

Behaviour

The Childwise Monitor, an annual survey of around 2,000 five to 16-year-olds in the UK, looks at media consumption, purchasing and social habits as well as key behaviour. It found that the majority of girls aged 15 to 16 think they are healthy and happy, but a quarter say they are unhealthy while one in five admit they are not happy most of the time. The vast majority of teenage girls, nine out of ten, had at times felt stressed about school work or experienced anxiety. Nearly 80 per cent said they sometimes felt inadequate while three-quarters had felt the need to lose weight, it said. This year we may be witnessing the impact of many years of campaigning, along with female success at both the London 2012 and Rio 2016 Olympics. 'Girls this age are the most likely to say they are unhealthy, and most likely to say they are unhappy a lot of the time,' said Mr Leggett. 'So, with more of them now taking part in sport at school, we could hope to see an improvement in their general well-being.'

24 January 2017

⇨ The above information is reprinted with kind permission from iNews. Please visit www.inews.co.uk for further information.

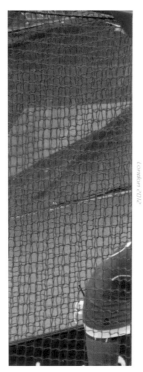

Is it time we legalise doping?

Following the Russian doping scandal, Lance Armstrong, Maria Sharapova, Justin Gatlin and other high-profile athletes, the topic of doping is dominating sport and poses a significant threat to its integrity. However, once we accept the fact that doping has always been a part of sport and that it may be impossible to completely eradicate, is it time to consider the idea of legalising doping?

The history of doping

Doping has existed in one way or another for as long as the Olympic Games have, stretching as far back as 776 BC. The term 'doping' stems from 'doop'; a drug used by the Ancient Greeks to enhance their sporting performance at a time when doping and match fixing was considered acceptable. The first rules against doping in sport were made as late as 1928, when the International Association of Athletics Federation (IAAF) banned doping for all of their athletes. Since then, improved procedures and technology to test performance-enhancing substances, it seems, have been successful in exposing athletes who choose to dope. However, recent findings suggest that only one in 30 athletes are ever caught in a doping test, even though many go through hundreds within their lifetime. Lance Armstrong took an estimated 500–600 tests, all of which were concluded to be clean. According to *Icarus*, the Oscar-nominated documentary, Armstrong was only caught as a result of his teammates choosing to testify against the cyclist.

Athletes have been doping to gain an advantage for as long as competitive sport has existed, with only a small percentage ever being found out. It's incredible to think of how many medals have been awarded to athletes, teams and nations who have been involved in doping, right under our noses, without us having a clue. I think the reason that we find this truth so upsetting is because sport is meant to provide an even playing field for all athletes and that it unites people in the common interest of sharing a fair and honest competition. It seems to me however, that if our reason for not tolerating doping is the desire to make sport fair, then maybe we need to consider the prospect of legalising doping.

Could doping make sports fairer?

The argument surrounding the fairness of sport goes beyond doping. In recent years we've seen the reputation of athletes being challenged because they are simply genetically superior or more naturally talented than others. There are also complaints that more economically developed nations also have a clear advantage over others. Just a few days ago, a BBC pundit covering the Winter Olympics in Pyeongchang complained about the unfair advantage other nations had over Great Britain due to the availability of funding and world-class facilities. So in the inherently unfair world of sport, could the accessibility and affordability of performance-enhancing drugs close the gap?

The problem with doping is that it brings morality into question. The general consensus is that doping challenges the core values of sport, but how is it any different to an athlete taking advantage of pioneering training and recovery techniques, or performance-related technologies to gain an advantage? The use of Hypoxic Air Tents for example, is considered legal in many sports. Athletes can use them to increase haematocrit levels, which in turn increases the oxygen-carrying capacity in your blood. This boosts the production of red blood cells, much in the same way as the banned drug erythropoietin (EPO) does. This type of equipment, like a lot of 'legal' performance-enhancing techniques and technologies, is expensive and therefore only available to those who can afford it.

While sport often drills down to natural ability, many athletes wouldn't have been as successful if they didn't have significant resources dedicated to their development. Even with clean athletes, the idea of sporting equality is slightly warped as there is a clear correlation between sporting success and how much of a nation's wealth is dedicated to it. British Cycling's growth over the past 18 years is a prime example of this. Since 2000 and the Sydney Olympics, British Cycling has seen its funding increase from £5.4 million to over £30 million for the Olympic and Paralympic Games in Rio de Janeiro. These investments have resulted in 24 state-of-the-art facilities and the creation of world-leading performance programmes for elite athletes. The knock-on effect is for all to see, with the Olympic and Paralympic cycling teams going from winning two Gold, two Silver and four Bronze in 2000 to 18 Gold, six Silver and eight Bronze in 2016. Given the influence that investment tends to have on performance, we can safely say that inequality in sport inherently exists. Wealthier nations can invest much more in sport to help athletes push their bodies to world-beating standards. The idea that an anti-doping stance preserves the fairness of sport is clearly inaccurate, and doping could be viewed as just another tool to maximise the abilities of an athlete.

The fact that performance-enhancing drugs are widely available and affordable (in relative terms to legal performance-enhancing techniques and technology) could mean that less economically developed nations are able to achieve results on par with their wealthier adversaries. Whilst this is an interesting concept it's perhaps a 'two wrongs doesn't make a right' argument, and we should be looking at eliminating financial factors in sport instead. The risk that an open-door policy to doping may pose is a trickle-down effect to grassroots whereby a lack of education and substance abuse could lead to wider arguments around the safety of athletes.

Could doping make sports safer?

Outside of the sporting world, the moral stance on drug use is changing to make it safer. Take Portugal for example, who 17 years ago decriminalised drug use and now records just three drug overdose deaths for every 1 million citizens, the second lowest of any European country. Given that Portugal has had such success, there is no reason why this logic couldn't be applied to the sporting world. However, there is one crucial difference between recreational and sporting drug use; the element of competition and the value that sporting success holds. The fact that athletes are taking drugs to gain a competitive advantage means that they are likely to push their bodies beyond what are considered natural

limits. This is a very different motivation to regular drug use, whereby athletes become reliant on drugs to retain a certain level of performance.

Although, just because athletes take drugs in the interest of competition, this does not mean that all drug use could not be safe. In Julian Savulescu's 'A Doping Manifesto', he positions 'safe doping' in a scenario whereby athletes are tested for physiological values (e.g. testosterone and haematocrit) rather than the variety of banned substances. The benchmark for a pass or fail would then become what are deemed safe levels of these physiological values. Sauvlescu's theory does hit a grey area as he explains 'dangerous' substances would still be outlawed. Who makes the decision between which drugs are considered safe and which are considered dangerous is another thing. Having said that, this could provide a doping culture with safety at the forefront, in contrast to the current anti-doping culture where only two per cent of dirty athletes are caught, and are potentially greatly harming their bodies.

However, regardless of what medical professionals deem to be 'safe', there is also a risk of the unknown that comes with doping. Not enough is known about the extent to which the abuse of performance-enhancing drugs damages the body. The World Anti-Doping Agency (WADA) has produced a list of health issues associated with doping, discussing the most common substances and the myths surrounding them, suggesting that doping always poses health risks. Given the amount of uncertainty around drug use for sporting purposes, a significant amount of expertise and resource is required to ensure the athlete is protected and remains healthy. Reverting to my previous point of inequality in sport, it is clear those at the top are the ones who will benefit the most, as someone like Lance Armstrong had a team of staff dedicated to helping him perform at his best with the least possible health risks. At grassroots level however, there is little control over who takes what, how they take it and how much they take. The lack of information could be incredibly dangerous and pose serious

risks to the athletes involved. Given that safety is a crucial factor for a sport to be universally popular, incidents resulting from doping could create dire consequences for participation levels. We are already seeing concerns over health come to the fore in many sports including American Football players and the health problems that come with concussions, as well as concerns on children heading the ball in football, and the age-long debate about boxing and brain damage to name a few. If doping becomes common practice is it likely that it will be next on the list?

Another important concern is that those who choose to compete without any performance-enhancing substances are left with the dilemma of either taking drugs or give up on their sporting aspirations. This is an ethical problem that seems extremely unfair on clean athletes, as doping will always pose certain health risks, and the option should not be to either risk one's health or give up a lifelong dream of competing.

The future of sport

The biggest threat that the legalisation of doping holds is the complete loss of the sports industry's integrity. People's love for sport derives from the idea that anything is possible; that people from all backgrounds and cultures can become sporting stars, and that underdogs can upset the elite. If doping becomes public knowledge, and common practice, we face the potential of complete disillusionment with sport. Considering its power to do good, I think we can all agree that this is a risk that sport simply cannot afford to take, but what is the solution to its oldest vice?

13 February 2018

⇨ The above information is reprinted with kind permission from Sport:80. Please visit www.sport80.com for further information.

Cobalt does not help a racehorse run faster, says trainer Mark Johnston

Robin Bastiman was banned for three years for injecting cobalt.

By Chris Cook

Cobalt doping does not improve a racehorse's performance, according to Mark Johnston, who will shortly become the most successful British trainer by number of wins. Johnston, a qualified vet, was speaking in the wake of a three-year ban given to Robin Bastiman for injecting a horse with a substance containing cobalt on a day when it was due to race.

'I do not believe for one second that it makes them run faster,' said Johnston, when asked about cobalt, which is thought by some to delay the onset of fatigue by stimulating production of red blood cells. 'There is mixed evidence and different opinions on whether it is of any benefit to humans. Even if it is, why should it work in horses? Why should blood doping work in horses, or EPO, or training at altitude?

'The horse has no shortage of red cells. It's got 40% spare in its spleen, it injects them under pressure, it doesn't need more oxygen-carrying capacity. That's not the limiting factor on getting oxygen to its muscles.

'We all know about wind problems and so on, but as much oxygen as you can deliver to those lungs, the circulatory system will carry it to the muscles and it'll carry it fast, faster than any other species. It's got the most incredible circulatory system, so why would any idiot want to give them cobalt? And yet people do, they'll give them whatever some clown tells them is going to make them run faster.'

But Johnston does not see cobalt's ineffectiveness as any kind of mitigation for Bastiman. 'He was injecting stuff into the horse in the belief that it was going to make it run faster. So even if it was water, it was still wrong.

'The most disappointing thing is the ignorance of people who will give things to horses with no evidence that it's going to make them go any quicker. They're all looking for something to turn lead into gold.'

Johnston noted that the Australian trainer Peter Moody, with whom he has had verbal sparring matches through the media, was banned for six months after an elevated cobalt level was found in one of his horses. Moody has since decided against returning to training. 'I've got no sympathy for him,' Johnston said. 'They shouldn't give him his licence back.'

Some of Moody's quotes have taken on an added significance since the ban and the Middleham trainer still remembers his outrage when the Australian was quoted as saying: 'If someone like Mark Johnston wants to train like they did 200 years ago, then good luck to him. You've got to look at every advantage within the rules. Obviously he doesn't have a vet in his yard.'

15 August 2018

⇨ The above information is reprinted with kind permission from *The Guardian*. Please visit www.theguardian.com for further information.

Anabolic steroid misuse

Anabolic steroids are prescription-only medicines that are sometimes taken without medical advice to increase muscle mass and improve athletic performance.

If used in this way, they can cause serious side effects and addiction.

Anabolic steroids are manufactured drugs that mimic the effects of the male hormone testosterone. They have limited medical uses and aren't to be confused with corticosteroids, a different type of steroid drug that's commonly prescribed for a variety of conditions.

This article explains the dangers of misusing anabolic steroids, and aims to advise and support those who are addicted to the drugs. It covers:

⇨ anabolic steroids and the law

⇨ why people misuse anabolic steroids

⇨ how they are taken

⇨ side effects

⇨ addiction

⇨ getting help.

Are anabolic steroids illegal?

Anabolic steroids are class C drugs, which can only be sold by pharmacists with a prescription.

It's not illegal to possess anabolic steroids for personal use. They can also be imported or exported, as long as this is carried out in person. This means they can't be posted or delivered by a courier or freight service.

However, it's illegal to possess, import or export anabolic steroids if it's believed you're supplying or selling them. This includes giving them to friends. The penalty is an unlimited fine, or even a prison sentence.

In professional sport, most organisations ban anabolic steroid use and test competitors for banned steroids.

Why people misuse anabolic steroids

Anabolic steroids are performance-enhancing drugs that increase muscle mass and decrease fat, as well as causing many undesirable effects. Some athletes, weightlifters and bodybuilders take them regularly to improve their physical performance and build up their bodies.

However, people of all ages have been known to misuse these drugs, including adolescent boys who suffer from body dysmorphia, an anxiety disorder where the way someone thinks about their body doesn't match the way it looks.

Teenage boys and young men may take the drugs because they have reverse anorexia. This is when they don't see themselves as being physically big enough or strong enough.

Some people believe taking anabolic steroids will help them become fit and healthy. This isn't true: taking anabolic steroids is a dangerous drug habit.

How anabolic steroids are taken

Anabolic steroids are usually injected into the muscle, but some are available in tablet form, or as creams or gels that are applied to the skin.

Most people who use anabolic steroids are aware of the dangers of taking them, and have ways of getting the desired effect without the undesirable side effects.

This involves injecting the drugs for a period of time and then stopping for a rest period before starting again. This is known as 'cycling'.

More than one type of anabolic steroid may be used at a time. Users believe this increases the effectiveness, and is known as 'stacking'.

The term 'pyramiding' refers to a combination of both stacking and cycling. One or more anabolic steroids are taken in a low dose. This is gradually increased to a maximum dose over six to 12 weeks, before the dose is reduced to zero to give the body a break and the cycle is started again.

Users tend to exercise more when they're taking high doses to make the most of their improved performance during this time.

Athletes have been known to try to time their injections so the drug is out of their system by the time they're drug tested.

Side effects of anabolic steroids

Regularly taking anabolic steroids causes a range of male features, not just increased muscle mass. It can also lead to potentially dangerous medical conditions, such as high blood pressure (hypertension) or heart attacks.

Physical effects

Effects of anabolic steroids in men can include:

⇨ reduced sperm count

⇨ infertility

⇨ shrunken testicles

⇨ erectile dysfunction

⇨ baldness

⇨ breast development

⇨ increased risk of developing prostate cancer

⇨ severe acne

⇨ stomach pain.

In women, anabolic steroids can cause:

⇨ facial hair growth and body hair

⇨ loss of breasts

⇨ swelling of the clitoris

⇨ a deepened voice

⇨ an increased sex drive

⇨ problems with periods

⇨ hair loss

⇨ severe acne.

In addition, both men and women who take anabolic steroids can develop any of the following medical conditions:

⇨ heart attack or stroke

⇨ liver or kidney tumours

⇨ high blood pressure (hypertension)

⇨ blood clots

⇨ fluid retention

⇨ high cholesterol

⇨ psychological effects.

Misusing anabolic steroids can also cause the following psychological or emotional effects:

⇨ aggressive behaviour

⇨ mood swings

⇨ manic behaviour

⇨ hallucinations and delusions.

Stunted growth in adolescents

Anabolic steroids accelerate bone growth, so if they're misused by adolescents who haven't yet had the growth spurt associated with puberty, the drugs can cause premature ageing of the bones and restricted growth.

Sharing needles

As anabolic steroids are often injected, there are risks associated with sharing needles. These are the same risks associated with recreational drug use, and include:

⇨ damage to veins, leading to ulcers or gangrene

⇨ hepatitis B infection

⇨ hepatitis C infection

⇨ HIV transmission.

Addiction

Like many other substances, anabolic steroids are addictive. This means you can crave the drug, require more to get the same effect, and have withdrawal symptoms if you suddenly stop taking them.

A person who is addicted to anabolic steroids will continue using them despite experiencing unpleasant physical side effects.

When doctors prescribe steroid medication, they always advise coming off the medication slowly by gradually reducing the dose. Coming off anabolic steroids suddenly can result in withdrawal symptoms that include:

⇨ depression and apathy

⇨ feelings of anxiety

⇨ difficulty concentrating

⇨ insomnia

⇨ anorexia

⇨ decreased sex drive

⇨ extreme tiredness (fatigue)

⇨ headaches

⇨ muscle and joint pain.

Getting help

You should see your GP if you think you're addicted to anabolic steroids. Treatment for an addiction to anabolic steroids will be similar to that of other types of addiction.

Your GP may refer you to a specially trained drugs counsellor. They'll discuss your addiction with you, how to safely stop taking steroids, and any obstacles you may face when trying to stop, plus strategies for dealing with those obstacles.

30 August 2018

⇨ The above information is reproduced with kind permission from the NHS. Please visit www. nhs.uk for further information.

© Crown Copyright 2018

UK anti-doping receives £6-million funding boost

Budget increased in the run up to Tokyo 2020 to cement UKAD's position as one of the leading anti-doping agencies in the world.

From: Department for Digital Culture, Media and Sport, UK Anti-Doping and Tracey Crouch, MP

⇨ Investment of £6.1 million will help educate athletes, share intelligence and conduct testing in the fight against drug cheats to keep sport clean.

⇨ Sports Minister Tracey Crouch also publishes second annual update on government's sport strategy that shows progress on governance.

UK Anti-Doping is to receive an additional £6 million of funding from the Government to further strengthen its armoury in the fight against doping, Sports Minister Tracey Crouch announced today.

The move comes after the first full-scale review of the organisation since it was set up in 2009 that has resulted in a number of recommendations to help make further progress in anti-doping.

These include:

⇨ UKAD to consider submitting a framework to government and sports to allow doping control officers to have unfettered access to conduct random testing at competitions

⇨ UKAD to encourage greater collaboration from law enforcement agencies and to ensure whistleblowers have confidence to come forward

⇨ Sports in receipt of public funding to report annually on their anti-doping education programmes to UKAD and publish this information on their websites

⇨ Health harms associated with the abuses of Image and Performance Enhancing Drugs (IPEDs) should be integrated into drug information and education supported by Public Health England, Public Health Wales, Health Scotland, Public Health (Northern Ireland)

and the Home Office Drugs Strategy

⇨ Government should revise the National Anti-Doping Policy by September 2018 in consultation with UKAD and the Home Country Sport Councils

⇨ UKAD to ensure that all publicly funded athletes and support personnel participate in annual anti-doping education programmes

⇨ UKAD to establish an Innovations Committee later this year to signpost new trends in doping

⇨ A new international strategy to be drawn up by UKAD to help drive a global approach to innovation in anti-doping.

The move means that over the next two years UKAD's budget will be increased by around 50 per cent to help it implement the recommendations in the tailored review.

Sports Minister Tracey Crouch said:

'We must do all we can to make sure sport is free from doping and that players and fans are confident that there is a level playing field. This £6-million additional funding for UKAD will help us take the fight even harder to those trying to cheat through doping. It will also help educate people at all levels of sport about the dangers of image and performance-enhancing drugs and maintain UKAD's standing as one of the leading anti-doping agencies in the world.'

UKAD will now work with the DCMS on the specifics of what the additional £6.1 million will be spent on.

UK Anti-Doping Chair Trevor Pearce said:

'We are delighted at the news from DCMS today, to significantly increase the funding available to UKAD for the next two years. This clear commitment to clean sport from government will allow us to increase the effectiveness of our current investigation, testing and education programmes, and also importantly to expand our investment into new approaches in the fight against doping. We look

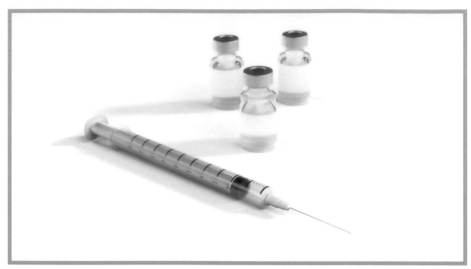

forward to working with DCMS on the implementation of recommendations for UKAD and we share their ambition for the UK to lead the world in Anti-Doping.'

Today Tracey Crouch has also published the second annual report to Parliament on the government's sport strategy 'Sporting Future'. Progress made on the implementation of the strategy includes:

⇨ Code for Sports governance being adhered to by national governing bodies to ensure greater transparency, accountability and diversity across the sector

⇨ Continued investment in the sector in line with the change in approach to encouraging participation in sport and physical activity that Sporting Future signalled. Sport England has invested over £530 million of exchequer and lottery money in over 2,500 projects over the past 20 months and is working with a broader range of organisations to get people active.

⇨ Sports Business Council set up, co-chaired by Tracey Crouch and Premier League executive chairman Richard Scudamore

⇨ Review of criminalisation of doping completed with recommendations made to strengthen approach to anti-doping

⇨ Held roundtables on the issue of mental health in physical activity and sport with work ongoing to make progress in this area

⇨ *Duty of Care in Sport* report published by Baroness Tanni Grey-Thompson to help the sector focus on what more can be done to ensure safeguarding of participants at every level

⇨ Successfully hosted major global sporting events including the 2017 World Athletics Championships

⇨ Won the right to host the 2022 Commonwealth Games in Birmingham.

Tracey Crouch added:

'We are making good progress on a number of fronts. We are ensuring our governing bodies have world leading standards of governance as well as targeting funding to encourage new participants in sport and physical activity. There is still more work to do. This year I will particularly focus on mental health in sport and encouraging the sector to continue to step up on safeguarding all participants – from the grassroots to the elite.'

30 January 2018

⇨ The above information is reprinted with kind permission from Department for Digital Culture, Media and Sport. Please visit www.gov.uk for further information.

Blows not concussion cause brain disease, according to new research

The effects of repeat concussion injuries on athletes, particularly American football and rugby players, is one of the biggest concerns in competitive sports today. However, a new Oxford University collaboration suggests that blows to the head can cause lasting trauma – even in the absence of signs of concussion.

By Robin Cleveland

The findings suggest that attempts to monitor and prevent concussions in sport, such as new designs for helmets, may be futile, since nothing can change the motion of head movement inflicted by a flying tackle.

Published in the journal *Brain*, the research identified early signs of the brain disease Chronic Traumatic Encephalopathy (CTE) after head injuries. The signs of the disease not only persisted long after the initial injury, but spread through the brain. The study provides the most conclusive evidence to date that it is repeated head impacts, such as tackles – even mild ones, and not concussion, that causes the disease.

CTE is a neurodegenerative disease triggered by a build-up of the protein tau around small blood cells in the brain. The condition is known to limit cognitive ability and cause brain cell death and dementia. The relationship between CTE and sports-related brain injury is widely known, but exactly which injuries can cause the disease, and whether concussion is one of them, is less clear.

Researchers from the Oxford University Institute of Biomedical Engineering worked in collaboration with 40 international partners on the project. The team, led by Boston University and including the Cleveland Clinic, Harvard Medical School and Lawrence Livermore National Laboratory, has carried out extensive studies over the past few years, comparing analysis of the brains of human teenagers with recent head injury, against mouse models. This work allowed the team to understand trauma to the brain both from military-related blast waves, with implications for military personnel, and impacts with implications for sports players. The work could support understanding of how head injuries can lead to CTE – particularly in young athletes and enable healthcare diagnostics and treatments, as well as preventative measures – such as adjustments to NFL and Rugby League protocol, to help those at risk of the disease and affected by head injury.

Professor Robin Cleveland of the Institute of Biomedical Engineering at Oxford University, a co-author on the work, said: 'The current NFL concussion protocol has already been under fire this season after a number of players returned to the field when perhaps they should not have; our work suggests that even a robust assessment of concussion may not be sufficient to determine damage may have occurred.'

The team's most recent study compared injuries caused by blast waves and blows to the head in the sports field. In the mouse tests, both the blast wave and the sports injury resulted in long-term brain damage (CTE), but only the blow to the head resulted in concussion. This suggests that CTE is not directly caused by concussion, but that both can lead to brain damage.

Computer simulations then investigated how the physical impact of each hit causes biological effect. It was found that both injuries resulted in high acceleration of the head. However, only head impacts resulted in direct mechanical damage of tissue which is likely responsible for concussion.

Their mechanistic studies were consistent with comparative analysis of four post-mortem brains from teenage athletes who had sustained closed-head impact injuries. The study revealed various signs of trauma in each brain, including one case of early-stage CTE and two cases of an abnormal presence of tau protein. By comparison, brains from four age-matched athletes that had not sustained recent head injury showed no evidence of these changes.

Professor Cleveland said: 'We have demonstrated that a blow to the head results in at least two different pathways to brain damage: one associated with acceleration of the head that results in CTE – a chronic effect that is associated with a range of neurological effects, from memory loss, to depression and suicide. The second is associated with the generation of damage to the brain tissue, which correlates with concussion.'

Dr Lee Goldstein, MD, PhD, an associate professor at the Boston University

School of Medicine and College of Engineering, said: 'The concussion is the red herring here. Our results may explain why approximately 20 per cent of athletes with CTE never suffered a diagnosed concussion. These findings provide strong evidence – the best evidence so far, that subconcussive impacts are not only dangerous but also causally linked to CTE.

'There are many players who are hit, who are hurt and who aren't getting help because it's clear that they're not at the level of concussion. Their brains are not in good shape and they go on to the next hit and the next one.'

18 January 2018

⇨ The above information is reprinted with kind permission from the University of Oxford. Please visit www.ox.ac.uk for further information.

Anxious Chinese parents cause gene testing boom as they try to discover young children's talents

By Neil Connor

When Fan Yimei's 11-year-old son gave up on his chess lessons to focus on fencing instead, she knew there was no point pressuring him to change his mind.

That's because she was told months before that he would excel in sports, while more studious past times were not in his DNA.

Her son is one of thousands of children in China who have undergone genetic testing which purportedly 'reveal' what talents they will develop in later life.

'My two baby boys were also tested, and I was told they'd be good at painting,' said Mrs Fan, who is from the eastern province of Zhejiang. 'So I'm just going to focus on art lessons for them.'

The trend in lab testing, which is prompted by pushy parents seeking to give their offspring an advantage, has seen the emergence of a growing number of 'health institutes' that claim to predict if children as young as a year old will be the next Mo Farah, Lady Gaga or Stephen Hawking.

The institutes charge hundreds of pounds to perform the tests, which involve taking a saliva swab that is then sent to laboratories. About two weeks later, parents are told whether their child is gifted in areas such as dancing, mathematics or painting.

Parents are also given a profile of their child's general level of intelligence, emotional understanding and concentration, and are told whether they will be introverted or extroverted.

The 'talent detecting' industry has emerged in China after the growth of a global industry which claims to be able to predict the future sporting prowess of youngsters through genetic testing.

Experts are highly skeptical of the scientific evidence to support such techniques, and ethical concerns have been raised over the right of children to have an open future.

But business is booming at 1Gene health institute in Hangzhou, Zhejiang, according to Wang Junyi, the company's president.

'Thousands' of children have done tests at the facility since it formally launched in October, Mr Wang said, due to a rising tide of parents that are desperate to choose wisely over their child's learning.

China scrapped the one child policy last year, but most families have just a single offspring who is often expected to support their older relatives when they reach adulthood.

This results in many parents – or so-called 'Tiger Mums' – being strict, or spending huge amounts on extra-curricular courses in the hope that children might achieve success in a specific field.

Mr Wang said: 'Many of my friends are anxious about deciding what their children should learn, as they fear making stupid decisions could result in lost opportunities.

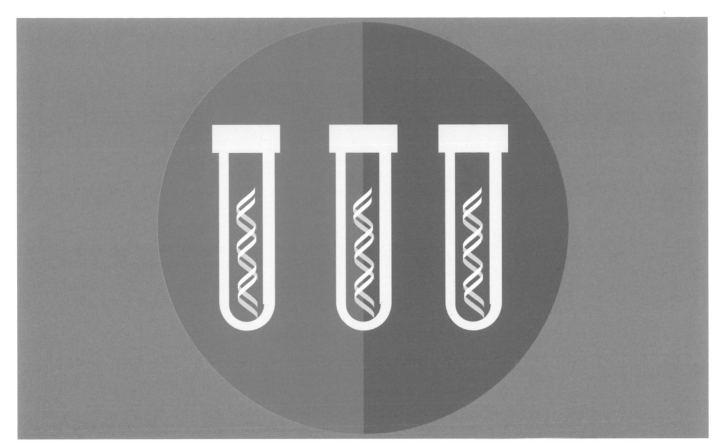

'They will be wasting money and destroying their children's confidence if they push them into something they are not good at, and this is where genetic testing can help.'

Other institutes to have emerged in China include Beijing-based HiGene, which reportedly had more than 1,500 customers in its first three months after it opened last year, and also Martime Gene company, from the eastern Shandong province.

Martime, which is expanding across the country, charges 2,000 yuan (£233) for a test which identifies talents in 20 areas, including dancing, mathematics and sports, while at 1Gene a talent test costs 3,999 yuan (£465) and a test predicting health problems is 2,999 yuan (£349). Other centres can charge up to £1,000.

The manager of Martime, who gave his surname as Dang, said geneticists compare results from children with a national genebank and findings from foreign experts.

'If the person has a similar gene to a gene we know reveals certain talents, we can tell the child also has those talents,' he said.

Mr Dang pointed to one success story of a boy who was told by the institute he had special singing talents, and he is now a student of Leo Ku, one of Asia's most famous performers.

But there are also parents who are given less positive results, such as Zhou Xian, who was told by 1Gene that her one-year-old daughter could become depressed and suffer from bad eyesight.

'I think it could be accurate. I have found my daughter has a bad temper and is very stubborn,' she said.

For Chang Zisong, an expert in genealogy at the Tianjin International Joint Academy of Biomedicine, such predictions are 'meaningless'.

'The primary reason that China doesn't outlaw these institutes is because by doing so would suggest that they have scientific value,' he told *The Telegraph*.

The growing ranks of 'talent spotters' in China, however, see it as the natural successor to sports testing, where labs analyse genes which are thought to have links with athletic abilities.

Mike McNamee, a Professor of Applied Ethics at Swansea University, said that industry is fast emerging and potentially highly lucrative, but those who believe in such testing are 'gullible'.

'Talent spotting is a gross over-simplification and overblown belief in the power of genetic technology wrapped up in a commercial enterprise,' he said.

'If parents want to know if their kid is going to be a great sprinter, or a great whatever, then go and watch them!'

17 February 2017

⇨ The above information is reprinted with kind permission from *The Telegraph*. Please visit www.telegraph.co.uk for further information.

Academics call for tackles and scrums to be banned from school rugby games

'Put children's interests ahead of corporate rugby unions', urge researchers.

By Ella Pickover

Schools should ban 'harmful contact' from rugby games, experts have said.

In a new opinion piece published in a leading medical journal, academics said that tackles and scrums should be prohibited on school playing fields.

Allyson Pollock and Graham Kirkwood from the Institute of Health at Newcastle University argue that most injuries in youth rugby occur due to the collision elements of the game.

Writing in the *British Medical Journal (BMJ)*, they said that ministers should 'put the interests of the child before those of corporate professional rugby unions'.

Removing collision from school rugby is likely to 'reduce and mitigate the risk of injury' in pupils, they said.

They argue that a history of concussion is associated with the 'lowering of a person's life chances' across a number of measures including low educational achievement and premature death. Meanwhile, a head injury is linked to an increased risk of dementia, they added.

Citing previous research into sports injuries in youngsters, the pair argue that rugby, along with ice hockey and American football, have the highest concussion rates.

They said that rule changes in collision sports can 'make a difference', highlighting the Canadian ban on 'body checking' – where a player deliberately makes contact with an opposing player – in ice hockey for under- 13-year-olds.

Meanwhile, the evidence for other strategies to reduce concussion risk in contact sport – such as mouth guards – is 'weak', the article adds.

And in the UK 'teacher training in the skills of rugby are lacking, as is concussion awareness training,' the pair wrote.

The researchers called on the UK Chief Medical Officers to advise the UK Government to remove 'harmful contact' from the game.

In 2016, the nation's most senior medics rejected a call for a ban on tackling in youth rugby.

But Professor Pollock, who has been researching injuries and rugby injuries for more than ten years, and senior research associate Mr Kirkwood said that under United Nations conventions, governments have a 'duty to protect children from risks of injury'.

'We call on the Chief Medical Officers to act on the evidence and advise the UK Government to put the interests of the child before those of corporate professional rugby unions and remove harmful contact from the school game,' they wrote.

'Most injures in youth rugby are because of the collision elements of the game, mainly the tackle.

'In March 2016, scientists and doctors from the Sport Collision Injury Collective called for the tackle and other forms of harmful contact to be removed from school rugby. The data in support of the call is compelling.'

Commenting on the article, Professor Tara Spires-Jones, UK Dementia Research Institute programme lead and deputy director of the Centre for Discovery Brain Sciences at the University of Edinburgh, said: 'Very strong, reproducible evidence supports a greater risk of dementia in people who have head injuries in their lifetimes, which urges caution in games where there is a significant risk of head injury.

'However, the data on specifically whether playing rugby or other contact sports in school increases your risk of dementia are not as robust yet due to a lack of large prospective studies. It is also very clear that there are many health risks of leading a sedentary lifestyle.'

A Department for Education spokeswoman said: 'Schools have the flexibility to offer a diverse PE curriculum which suits the needs of their students.

'We expect schools to be aware of all of the risks associated with sporting activities and to provide a safe environment for pupils.

'There is expert advice available for schools on how to manage activities safely and reduce the risk of injuries and accidents. On top of this, staff should be given the information and training they need to manage risks effectively.'

26 September 2017

⇨ The above information is reprinted with kind permission from The Press Association Please visit www.independent.co.uk for further information.

Scrums and tackling 'should be banned' in school rugby

By Laura Donnelly, Health Editor

Tackling and scrums should be banned in school rugby, to protect children from the risk of concussion and later brain damage, academics say.

Writing in the *British Medical Journal*, they urged the UK's Chief Medical Officers CMOs) to 'put the interests of the child' first and remove potentially harmful contact from the game.

The opinion piece cites research suggesting it is far more dangerous than other sports, increasing the risk of violent behaviour and dementia.

One New Zealand study of insurance claims found an occasional game of rugby is 500 times as risky as regular cycling.

Another study comparing a range of sports found concussion rates in rugby were three times more than those of ice hockey, and eight times those of American football.

Head injuries have been linked to an increased risk of dementia, neuro-degenerative conditions such as Parkinson's disease and to violent behaviour.

Professor Allyson Pollock, director of the Institute of Health and Society at Newcastle University, and co-author Graham Kirkwood, said changes in sports rules to ban intentional body contact had been shown to dramatically improve safety.

In 2013, Canada introduced a ban on 'body checking' – intentional body contact – in under 13s rugby. Research found it reduced the risk of concussion by two-thirds, the authors said.

In July 2016, the four UK CMOs rejected the call for a ban on tackling in youth rugby, citing a report which claimed rugby was no more injury prone than other sports.

But Professor Pollock and Mr Kirkwood say – under the United Nations Convention on the Rights of the Child (Article 19) – 'governments have a duty to protect children from risks of injury and to ensure the safety of children, which is why we are calling on CMOs to act now.'

The experts' concerns have been raised as the RFU (Rugby Football Union) is running a programme of introducing the sport to a million children in state schools across England, which is due to finish in 2019.

Professor Pollock and Mr Kirkwood, a former NHS nurse who is now a senior research associate in the Institute of Health and Society, said most injuries are because of the collision elements of the game – mainly the tackle.

Professor Pollock said: 'We call on the CMOs to act on the evidence and advise the UK Government to put the interests of the child before those of corporate professional rugby unions and remove harmful contact from the school game.'

They said collision sports are where 'athletes purposely hit or collide with each other or with inanimate objects – including the ground – with great force'.

The authors cited research showing rugby had the highest concussion rates in children – 4.18 per 1,000 athlete exposures compared to 1.20 and 0.53 for ice hockey and American football, respectively.

A New Zealand study combining injury insurance claims data with data from a range of surveys found that playing rugby – one game every three weeks – was 460 to 530 times more dangerous than a half-hour cycle ride trip three times a week.

Professor Pollock said: 'It's well recognised children are vulnerable and require specific measures to control the unique risks associated with this group.

'The call for a cautionary approach and the removal of collision from school rugby and to end compulsion in the school game is likely to reduce and mitigate the risk of injury in school children.'

But others questioned the recommendation.

Dr Alan Carson, Reader in Neuropsychiatry, University of Edinburgh, said that while removing contact sports would cut injury risks, it was 'far from proven' that concussion caused problems in later life.

'There is no doubt sport and exercise are good for you and that effect is far more important in terms of all cause mortality than any increase in risk of neurodegeneration,' he said.

'The health crisis facing Britain's children is not concussion but obesity and lack of exercise. Public health clinicians should think very carefully before calling for measures that may cut participation in sport.'

26 September 2017

⇨ The above information is reprinted with kind permission from *The Telegraph*. Please visit www.telegraph.co.uk for further information.

Food and drinks for sport

Find out what food and drink will help you get the most out of your sport and fitness activities.

You should aim to eat a healthy, balanced diet whatever your activity level, as this will provide you with all the nutrients you need.

If you need specialist nutrition advice, contact the Sport and Exercise Nutrition Register (SENr).

The Eatwell Guide shows you how much you should eat from each food group to get the balance right.

Food for energy

Starchy and other forms of carbohydrate provide a source of energy for your body to perform at its best, no matter what your sport or activity.

In general, the more you exercise, the more carbohydrate you need to include in your daily meals and around exercise.

A demanding exercise regime will use up your stored energy from carbohydrate quickly, so include some carbohydrate in most of your meals.

A diet low in carbohydrate can lead to a lack of energy during exercise, loss of concentration and delayed recovery.

If you wish to adopt a lower carbohydrate diet for your sport, you should seek specialist advice.

Healthy sources of carbohydrate include:

⇨ wholegrain bread

⇨ wholegrain breakfast cereals (including some cereal bars)

⇨ brown rice

⇨ wholewheat pasta

⇨ potatoes (with skins on)

⇨ fruit, including dried and tinned fruit.

Food for muscles

Eating protein-rich foods alone won't build big muscles.

Muscle is gained through a combination of muscle-strengthening exercise, and a diet that contains protein and sufficient energy from a balance of carbohydrates and fats.

Not all the protein you eat is used to build new muscle. If you overeat protein, the excess will be used mostly for energy once your body has what it needs for muscle repair.

Most fitness enthusiasts can get enough protein from a healthy, varied diet without having to increase their protein intake significantly.

Healthy sources of protein:

⇨ beans, peas and lentils

⇨ cheese, yoghurt and milk

⇨ fish, including oily fish like salmon or mackerel

⇨ eggs

⇨ tofu, tempeh and other plant-based meat-alternatives

⇨ lean cuts of meat and mince

⇨ chicken and other poultry.

A source of protein should be included at most mealtimes to optimise muscle building.

Taking in protein before and after a workout has been shown to help kickstart the muscle repair process.

Training protein snacks:

⇨ milk of all types – but lower-fat types contain less energy

⇨ unsweetened soy drink

⇨ natural dairy yoghurt of all types – including Greek yoghurt and kefir

⇨ soy yoghurt and other plant-based alternatives

⇨ unsalted mixed nuts and seeds

⇨ unsweetened dried fruit

⇨ boiled eggs

⇨ hummus with carrot and celery sticks.

Food before sport and exercise

You should allow about three hours before you exercise after having a main meal, such as breakfast or lunch.

An hour before exercising, having a light snack that contains some protein, and is higher in carbohydrate and lower in fat, is a good choice to help you perform during your training and recover afterwards.

Choose a snack that you'll digest quickly, like:

⇨ porridge

⇨ fruit, such as a banana

⇨ a slice of wholegrain bread spread thinly with a nut butter

⇨ a plain or fruit scone with low-fat cheese

⇨ yoghurt or non-dairy alternatives

⇨ cottage cheese and crackers

⇨ a glass of milk or non-dairy alternatives.

Snacks to avoid before exercise

These types of food may cause stomach discomfort if eaten just before exercising.

Fatty foods, like:

⇨ chips or french fries

⇨ avocados

⇨ olives

⇨ crisps

⇨ full-fat cheeses

⇨ large amounts of nuts.

High-fibre foods, like:

⇨ raw vegetables

⇨ high-fibre cereals

⇨ raw nuts and seeds

Food and drink during exercise

Most exercise lasting less than 60 minutes only requires water.

If you're exercising for longer, have a quick-digesting carbohydrate and some electrolytes (salts and minerals), such as:

⇨ an isotonic sports drink

⇨ a glass of milk

- ⇨ a banana
- ⇨ dried fruit
- ⇨ a cereal or sports bar
- ⇨ carbohydrate gel

Make sure you're drinking enough water (or similar) during your effort.

Water and exercise

Not drinking enough water can have a major effect on your performance.

You should start any exercise session well hydrated. This means drinking water regularly throughout the day.

The choice of drink depends on the intensity and duration of the exercise, and your training goals.

In general:

- ⇨ only water is needed for moderate exercise that lasts less than an hour
- ⇨ an isotonic sports drink, milk, or a combination of high-carbohydrate food and water for hard sessions that last longer than an hour.

You can make a homemade sports drink with 200ml of squash (not low calorie), 800ml water and a large pinch of salt.

What to eat after exercise

Food and drink also plays a part in recovering effectively from training.

If you train several times a day, refuelling with a source of carbohydrate and protein – such as a glass of milk and a banana – within 60 minutes of finishing your first session can help you recover faster.

If you're training less than this or have more time to recover, make sure you rehydrate with water and eat as soon as you can afterwards. This might be your next main meal.

Food supplements and exercise

In general, a balanced diet will provide the nutrients and energy necessary for sport without the need for food supplements.

Athletes wanting to use supplements should seek specialist advice from a registered sports performance nutritionist from the Sport and Exercise Nutrition Register (SENr).

Exercise to lose weight

A demanding exercise routine can leave you feeling quite hungry if you're not refuelling correctly in between exercise sessions.

If you're trying to lose weight, you'll need to watch what you eat and drink after your workouts.

If you consume more energy than you burned during your exercise, you may find yourself putting on weight rather than losing it.

A punishing exercise routine may not be the best way to lose weight.

27 May 2017

- ⇨ The above information is reproduced with kind permission from the NHS. Please visit www.nhs.uk for further information.

© Crown Copyright 2018

Wearing protective headgear in rugby may increase the risk of serious injury – new research

THE CONVERSATION

An article from **The Conversation.**

By Andrew Barnes, Senior Lecturer in Sport and Exercise Science, Sheffield Hallam University

Rugby, with its rucks and its mauls, its scrums and its tackles, is considered one of the most physical sports played in schools.

Head injuries and concussions pose a serious threat to the welfare of young players. And research has shown that at youth level, on average between one and two players from each team will suffer a concussion every season. This is significantly higher than other contact sports such as ice hockey and American football.

The fears around concussion and head injuries in young players has led to calls for tackling to be banned at school level. It has also no doubt caused some parents to rush to the shops to buy protective headgear for their children to wear during games and training.

But as our recent research shows, wearing protective headgear may actually result in an increased risk of injury. This means that at the youth level, parents may insist on their child wearing headgear in the belief they are helping to reduce the injury risk, when in fact the opposite could be true.

Reckless tackling

Previous research already shows that although headgear may protect against minor superficial head injuries – such as lacerations and abrasions – it does not reduce the incidence of concussion.

Similarly, our new research, published in *BMJ Open Sport & Exercise Medicine* found that some rugby players seem to wear protective headgear to give them the confidence not to worry about getting injured. And that as a result, players may display reckless tackling behaviours that may increase the risk of serious injuries such as concussions.

But the issue of concussion in rugby is not just limited to the youth game. The highest incidence of rugby-related concussions is seen at the community or sub-elite level which is the largest section of adults who play rugby.

So if tackling was banned in schools, it could mean that many players choosing to play at this adult level may not have experienced fundamental coaching on how to tackle. This is an important point, because research based on South African youth players found that poor tackle technique is more likely to result in a tackle leading to a head injury.

Given this, and the fact that most injuries in rugby occur during the tackle (up to 64%), rather than an outright ban on tackling, strategies aimed at making the tackle safer appear to make the most sense.

Coaching the tackle

In this way, player and coach education strategies to reduce injury rates have been found to be effective – particularly with youth players. Most notably the RugbySmart scheme in New Zealand and the BokSmart scheme in South Africa. The two schemes share similar programme structures and aim to educate coaches and referees in an attempt to prevent serious injuries to players. The Boksmart intervention, for example, resulted in a 40% reduction in catastrophic injuries in a group of junior players.

Correct head placement, using the shoulder, and driving the legs in contact have all been found to be technique factors associated with a reduced risk of a concussive tackle. Which is why initiatives aimed at coaches, teachers and referees should focus on ensuring safe tackling behaviours are adopted and retained by youth players.

And positively, research has actually found that junior players value tackle training and the time spent on techniques to help reduce injury. This is encouraging because children who are taught correct technique from a young age are more likely to retain safe tackle behaviours if they continue to play rugby. And this of course helps to reduce injury rates, and makes the sport safer at all levels of the game.

24 October 2017

⇨ The above information is reprinted with kind permission from *The Conversation*. Please visit www.theconversation.com for further information.

All of the UK's links golf courses could disappear by 2100

By Alistair Dunsmuir

An alarming report from the UK's leading environmental organisation charity has found that every links golf course in the UK is in danger of disappearing in less than a century due to climate change.

The Climate Coalition says golf faces an 'unexpected threat' from even a slight rise in sea levels, and Open Championship venues such as St Andrews and Royal Troon could be under water by 2100.

The report, which adds that six of the UK's seven wettest years on record have occurred since 2000, predicts that 'golf courses will crumble into the sea'.

'Climate change is already impacting our ability to play and watch the sports we love,' said the report, adding that extreme weather is a factor in declining participation and lost revenue.

Last year we reported on the 455-year-old Montrose Golf Links, which was investigating the possibility of a crowdfunding campaign to raise £5 million to install rock armour alongside three of its seaside holes, following 25 years of coastal erosion.

Chris Curnin, director at Montrose Golf Links, said: 'As the sea rises and the coast falls away, we're left with nowhere to go. Climate change is often seen as tomorrow's problem – but it's already eating away at our course.

'In a perfect storm we could lose five to ten metres over just a couple of days and that could happen at pretty much any point.'

There was as much as 20 per cent less playing time for courses across the greater Glasgow area in 2016–17 compared to ten years earlier, the report suggests.

'These findings should cause great concern among golf's authorities,' said BBC golf correspondent Iain Carter.

'The game was founded on the links turf of the British seaside and provides golf in its most authentic form – as well as sums in excess of £75 million to local economies on an annual basis.

'But the sport has recognised its precarious position at the hands of mother nature, with a number of green initiatives adopted in recent years.

'This report might also impact on discussions aimed at limiting driving distances because it highlights potential dangers in maintaining the current trend of lengthening golf courses.'

'It is a fact that increased rainfall and extreme events are causing more disruption in recreational golf,' added Richard Windows of the Sports Turf Research Institute.

One in six Scottish golf courses are on the coast, where they are at the most risk of erosion due to rising sea levels, added the report.

Steve Isaac, director of golf course management at the R&A, said: 'There is no question it is becoming a huge factor.

'I believe golf is more impacted by climate change than any other sport aside from skiing.

'We are feeling it now with increases in unplayable holes, winter course closures and disruption to professional tournaments.

'And the future threats are very real.'

Professor Piers Forster, director of the Priestley International Centre for Climate at the University of Leeds, added: 'Climate change is already affecting the historic game of golf in its birthplace.

'Without cutting the carbon emissions driving climate change, sea levels will rise by over a metre and extremely wet winters will become the norm,' he warned.

'Many aspects of our lives including the game of golf would struggle to adapt to such a changed world.'

The Climate Coalition, which is made up of groups ranging from the National Trust and the Women's Institute to WWF, the RSPB, Greenpeace and Oxfam, is releasing the report as part of its 'Show The Love' campaign, which celebrates things people love but that could be lost due to climate change.

7 February 2018

⇨ The above information is reprinted with kind permission from *The Golf Business* which is published by Union Press Ltd. Please visit www.thegolfbusiness.co.uk for further information.

Key facts

- Over £2.5 million for new innovative medal support plans to provide National Lottery funding to world-level athletes in Badminton, Archery, Karate and Sport Climbing. (page 1)

  - Tokyo Olympic medal target range increased to 54–92 (from 51–85) (page 1)

  - Tokyo Paralympic medal target range increased to 119–168 (from 115–162) (page 1)

- The amount of physical activity you need to do each week is determined by your age. (page 12)

  - early childhood (under five years old) (page 12)

  - adults (19 to 64 years old) (page 12)

  - older adults (65 and over) (page 12)

- To maintain a basic level of health, children and young people aged five to 18 need to do: (page 12)

  - at least 60 minutes of physical activity every day – this should range from moderate activity, such as cycling and playground activities, to vigorous activity, such as running and tennis. (page 12)

  - on three days a week, these activities should involve exercises for strong muscles and bones, such as swinging on playground equipment, hopping and skipping, and sports such as gymnastics or tennis. (page 12)

- Around 63% of men were active in sport compared to 58% of women, based on the Active Lives Survey data for year ending May 2017. (page 16)

- The most popular physical activity among women was walking for leisure (24%) followed by fitness activities (19%) in May 2017. Men were the most active in general sporting activities (29% of men compared to just under 17% of women). (page 16)

- On average, 43% of people with a disability participated in sport activities for over 150 minutes a week in year ending May 2017. This was more than 20 percentage points lower than 65% of those with no disability. (page 16)

- Around 70% of individuals in managerial, administrative and professional occupations were active in sport in year ending May 2017. In contrast, around 49% of those long-term unemployed or never worked were active in sport. (page 16)

- In year ending May 2017, the most common activity was running (15%) followed by fitness class (14%) and gym (12%), ranked by proportion of population participating at least twice over the last 28 days prior to survey. (page 16)

- More than half (50/85) of female football and rugby union fans interviewed, suggested that sharing an interest in their sport gave people a common bond or connection with a person they had not met before. (page 22)

- Almost half (24/51) of football fans and nearly three-quarters (25/34) of rugby supporters across all age groups complained about numbers of women's toilets at old sports grounds and/or the 'abysmal' state of those facilities that did exist. (page 22)

- Anabolic steroids are class C drugs, which can only be sold by pharmacists with a prescription. (page 28)

  - In professional sport, most organisations ban anabolic steroid use and test competitors for banned steroids. (page 28)

- Investment of £6.1 million will help educate athletes, share intelligence and conduct testing in the fight against drug cheats to keep sport clean. (page 29)

- Starchy and other forms of carbohydrate provide a source of energy for your body to perform at its best, no matter what your sport or activity. (page 36)

- A diet low in carbohydrate can lead to a lack of energy during exercise, loss of concentration and delayed recovery. (page 36)

- Muscle is gained through a combination of muscle-strengthening exercise, and a diet that contains protein and sufficient energy from a balance of carbohydrates and fats. (page 36)

- A source of protein should be included at most mealtimes to optimise muscle building. (page 36)

- Taking in protein before and after a workout has been shown to help kickstart the muscle repair process. (page 36)

- Most exercise lasting less than 60 minutes only requires water. (page 36)

- Not drinking enough water can have a major effect on your performance. (page 37)

- An alarming report from the UK's leading environmental organisation charity has found that every links golf course in the UK is in danger of disappearing in less than a century due to climate change. (page 39)

- Six of the UK's seven wettest years on record have occurred since 2000, and it is predicted that 'golf courses will crumble into the sea'. (page 39)

- There was as much as 20 per cent less playing time for courses across the greater Glasgow area in 2016–17 compared to ten years earlier. (page 39)

- One in six Scottish golf courses are on the coast, where they are at the most risk of erosion due to rising sea levels. (page 39)

Glossary

Anabolic steroid

'Anabolic steroid' is a blanket term for drugs which mimic the effects of male reproductive hormones, i.e. by boosting muscle growth and protein synthesis. Side effects such as aggression, liver damage and high blood pressure can be very harmful. Some athletes take them illegally in order to improve their performance; people who use these performance-enhancing drugs in excess sometimes don't even view themselves as 'drug addicts', but rather that they are healthy people who are taking pride in their appearance.

Athlete

A highly-trained professional or amateur sportsperson.

Diuretic

A chemical that can be ingested by athletes, increasing the excretion of water from their body during urination. This is done in order to hide banned substances during urine tests, as urine is more diluted. Diuretic use in sporting competitions is illegal.

Doping

The use of performance-enhancing drugs by athletes during sporting competitions. Most of these drugs are illegal and players are required by law to take a drugs test before taking part in competitive events. If it is found that they have taken drugs they will automatically be disqualified from the event, and may also be banned from taking part in any future competitions for a specified period of time.

Elite athlete

A person who is currently or has previously competed as a varsity player (individual or team), a professional player or a national or international level player.

Fitness tracker

A wearable device that monitors fitness levels. Many of these devices track steps, heart rate, stairs climbed, sleep patterns, etc.

Gender pay gap

At EU level, the gender pay gap is defined as the relative difference in the average gross hourly earnings of women and men within the economy as a who

Hooliganism

A popular term in the past for violence at football matches. Match organisers have worked very hard in recent years to combat hooliganism. Police and other security measures are now routinely put in place to control rioting fans, and repeat 'football hooligans' can be banned from travelling abroad to attend games.

Inclusive sport

Sport which is inclusive does not discriminate on the grounds of gender, ethnicity, sexual orientation or disability. Sport is usually segregated where athletes have a physical difference which makes equal competition difficult – men and women do not generally compete against each other, for example, nor disabled and able-bodied athletes. This is called classification. However, there is no ban on any athlete competing in a separate competition. This is why the term 'sport equity' is sometimes used rather than equality. Athletes should be protected from discrimination and unfair treatment, such as racist and homophobic chanting at football matches.

Match-fixing

Match-fixing is a serious crime and is cheating. This is when someone purposely alters the outcome of a game in exchange for money (a bribe). For example, arranging the use of red and yellow cards or purposely playing poorly in order to throw a game.

Olympic Games

Every four years the Olympic Games are held in a different city around the world. The next summer Olympic Games, which will take place in 2020, are to be held in Tokyo.

Paralympic Games

The Paralympic Games are a series of sporting competitions open to athletes with physical disabilities. They are held immediately following the Olympic Games. Athletes with disabilities including amputations, paralysis and blindness take part in a wide range of competitive sports.

Rugby scrum

A scrum (short for scrummage) is a method of restarting play in rugby that involves players packing closely together with their heads down and attempting to gain possession of the ball. Depending on whether it is in rugby union or rugby league, the scrum is utilized either after an accidental infringement or when the ball has gone out of play.

Assignments

Braintstorming

- Brainstorm what you know about sport.
- What is doping?
- What is a paralympian?
- What is a fitness tracker?
- What are extreme sports?

Research

⇨ In pairs, do some research into the different types of fitness trackers currently on the market. What forms do they come in and what are they used to track? You should make notes on your findings and share with the rest of your class.

⇨ Do some research into the different types of sport in which paralympians can participate. Do the sports vary in different countries? Make some notes and share your findings with the rest of your class.

⇨ In small groups do some research into the ticket prices charged by various football clubs in the UK. Produce a graph to show your findings and share with the rest of your class.

⇨ Conduct a questionnaire amongst your classmates, friends and family to find out how much exercise they do each week. What are the different types of exercises done by different genders and age groups. Prepare a graph to demonstrate your findings.

⇨ In groups, do some research into golf clubs in the UK. Make a list of the ones you find and the membership costs per year. Produce a graph to show your findings.

⇨ In pairs, do some research into genetic testing, which claims to be able to predict the future sporting prowess of youngsters. Write a report which should fill one A4 page and share with your class.

Design

⇨ In groups, design a fitness tracker. What will it be called?

⇨ Design a poster to be displayed in public places such as school/college notice boards, to encourage more women to participate in sport.

⇨ In pairs, design a poster advertising a forthcoming football match.

⇨ In pairs, design a leaflet informing people about the types of food and drink which will help them to get the most out of their sport and fitness activities. It should give some details about where they can get further information on this matter.

⇨ In groups, choose a sport and design a new piece of protective equipment for participants to use. It could be to protect their heads, or maybe some part of their body. You should think of a suitable name for it.

⇨ Oral

⇨ Read the article on page 21 'Forbes' rich list shows sport fails to respect women – let alone pay them properly'. Split the class into two halves – boys versus girls. You should debate the issues raised in this article, the boys arguing against equality for women in sport and the girls arguing for.

⇨ As a class, discuss the issue of violence at football matches. What do you think are the causes and what could be done to combat this?

⇨ Create a PowerPoint presentation that explores the levels of exercise relevant to different age groups needed to maintain a basic level of health. You should consider what effects different exercises have on the body.

⇨ In pairs, go through the illustrations in this book and discuss what you think the artist was trying to portray. Would you have designed the illustration differently?

⇨ Read the article 'Is it time we legalise doping?' on page 25 and then split the class into two groups. One group should argue for legalising doping and the other should oppose it.

Reading/writing

⇨ Write a one-paragraph definition of an athlete.

⇨ Write a one-paragraph definition of the Olympic Games.

⇨ Imagine you are an agony Aunt/Uncle. A 12-year-old gymnast has written to you saying their coach is making inappropriate remarks to them and making them feel uncomfortable. They are too frightened to tell anyone and worried they might lose their place on the team if they do so. Write a suitable reply and give them advice on where they might find help and support.

⇨ Write a report for your school newspaper about the issue of 'tackling and scrums' during rugby games. You should write either from the point of view of agreeing with contact during games or being against contact.

⇨ Find out about the hike in season ticket prices being charged by football clubs. Write a report on this which should cover at least one A4 page.

⇨ Choose one of the articles from this book and write 300 words exploring the themes the author has chosen to depict.

Acknowledgements

The publisher is grateful for permission to reproduce the material in this book. While every care has been taken to trace and acknowledge copyright, the publisher tenders its apology for any accidental infringement or where copyright has proved untraceable. The publisher would be pleased to come to a suitable arrangement in any such case with the rightful owner.

Images

All images courtesy of iStock except pages 1, 4, 9, 13, 14, 23, 24, 35, and 39: Pixabay

Illustrations

Don Hatcher: pages 10 & 37. Simon Kneebone: pages 6 & 27. Angelo Madrid: pages 17 & 18

Additional acknowledgements

Page 31: Robin Cleveland, University of Oxford, https://doi.org/10.1093/brain.awx350. [Accessed September 2018]

With thanks to the Independence team: Shelley Baldry, Danielle Lobban, Jackie Staines and Jan Sunderland.

Tina Brand

Cambridge, October 2018